My journey concerning mental illness began at the age of nineteen. Life has led me in many different directions. Drastic mood swings greatly affected my professions. My successes as a film and television actor have been clouded by my experience in the United States Army. A complete mental upheaval occurred during the insanity of basic training, from which there seemed to be no return.

September 11, 2001, caused my unstable mind to collapse, very similar to the fractured Twin Towers as they splintered and fell. Suicide then became an alternative to life. Absolute self-destruction followed in a devastating manner. My life was forever altered in the brief second it took my heart to beat in one solitary, fateful moment.

Patterns began to reveal themselves, regarding my own annihilation. I was an unwilling patient of my doctor's sound advice and prescribed medications throughout my adult years. My ever-increasing failure to swallow the truth, metaphorically and literally, devoured my mental health. The end result was nothing less than chaos. My mind and body became *consumed* by my inability to heal from within.

Today, I have an insatiable thirst to regain the sanity of my blissful childhood. I have opened my hand to grasp firmly the possibilities of support systems. Mental stability is gaining momentum in my life. I did swallow my very necessary medications yesterday. The same willing process occurred again this morning. I hope to have the strength of will to consume the colorful pills tomorrow.

Todd Lawson LaTourrette

Consumed

Todd Lawson LaTourrette

Consumed

Vanguard Press

A CIP catalogue record for this title is
available from the British Library.

ISBN 978-1784651244

All names of the persons referred to within my memoir have been
changed, aside from my family, in order to protect the individuals and
their unquestionable honor.

Vanguard Press is an imprint of
Pegasus Elliot MacKenzie Publishers Ltd.
www.pegasuspublishers.com

First Published in 2016

Vanguard Press
Sheraton House Castle Park
Cambridge England

Printed & Bound in Great Britain

I wish to thank my family for their unending love, ceaseless support, and unwavering belief in me. There truly exist no sentiments that may fully describe the sincere love I feel for my mother and father. I am forever grateful.

Acknowledgements

I have survived my journey, thus far, due to the endless dedicated efforts of my family and psychiatrist. In addition, I will not understate the importance of my necessary prescribed medications, without which my past would truly be my present.

Contents

PRELUDE — 15

I. FIRST SIGNS — 17

THE JOURNEY BEGINS — 17
LES MISERABLES — 21

II. BEGINNING OF THE END — 26

SWEENEY TODD — 26
SUMMER STOCK — 31

III. NEWLY ACQUIRED SKILLS AND PATTERNS — 35

CARPENTRY — 35
SELF-MEDICATING — 38

IV. SELF-DESTRUCTIVE — 44

CUTTING — 44
WILL THE SUN COME OUT? — 47

V. MENTAL UPHEAVAL — 53

SKY DIVING — 53
THE WHOLE TRUTH AND NOTHING BUT? — 56

VI. INCARCERATION — 66

THE BRIG AND BIBLE — 66
A GIFT FROM GOD — 69

VII. CYCLING — 76

MOTORCYCLES 76
CRASH 81

VIII. TRUE LOVE 87

LAURA IN LAS VEGAS 87
DESTRUCTIVE LOVE 93

IX. DIAGNOSIS 95

MY BIPOLAR ILLNESS 95
TYPE II 97

X. END OF THE BEGINNING 102

SEPTEMBER 11TH, 2001 102
BIPOLAR, TYPE I 107

XI. PSYCHOTIC MIXED EPISODE 110

DELUSIONAL 110
PREPARATION FOR MY SALVATION 111

XII. THE AFTERMATH 119

REALITY OF MY ACTIONS 119
THERAPEUTIC LOVE 121
HELL 126

XIII. INCESSANT INQUIRIES 130

"WHAT HAPPENED TO YOUR HAND?" 130
A MUCH NEEDED ROMANCE 135

XIV. NORMALCY? 138

THE HAND 138
LYING 144

XV. SINKING FURTHER 149

CREDIT CARD DEBT   149
AUSTRALIA   152

XVI. A NECESSITY FOR MEDICATIONS   155

SIDE EFFECTS   155
SUICIDE AS AN ALTERNATIVE   159

XVII. LEARNING HOW TO LIVE   165

INSTITUTIONALIZED   165
MOTHERLY ADVICE   166

XVIII. ACTING   170

BUDDING FILM ACTOR   170
I COULD NOT SEE THE FOREST THROUGH THE TREES   177

XIX. MENTAL STABILITY   181

A NEW DESIRE TO MEDICATE   181
TRUTH, YES… AND NOTHING BUT.   184
A PASSION FOR LEARNING   185
FACING MY FEARS   188

XX. OVERCOMING VS. CHAOS   193

WATER   193
RELIVING THE PAST   194
A HAND, A HAND! MY KINGDOM…   198

XXI. NEW OPPORTUNITIES   202

OLD HABITS   202
SELF-LOVE   204

XXII. PAST, PRESENT…FUTURE   206

HONESTY AND FORGIVENESS   206

Prelude

I walked to the garage where my worm drive circular saw awaited me. I carefully placed the saw into the flimsy walls of my blue nylon sports duffel bag, and secretly re-entered my parent's home. The powerful tool lay caged, and hidden in my bedroom closet for two days. This fact was not due to any lack of my willful determination, however. My irrational reasoning, within my rational mind, chose the date carefully. Christmas Eve had always been a very special day in our family. We often enjoyed the festivities during a midnight candle service, or talked together while opening our Christmas presents. Christmas Eve was a night on which we withheld no emotions and truly cared for one another. I considered Christmas Eve to be pure with love, affection, and self-sacrifice.

I opened my closet door at eleven thirty p.m. in order to attain my resolute goal. I gently released the heavy and powerful circular saw from its blue nylon cage. I had planned the ritual for my salvation to the very last detail. There was no question in my delusional mind as to what I must do, and how I was going to accomplish the premeditated task.

I slowly exited my bedroom and proceeded to the living room fireplace, where I began to prepare my circular saw. I duct-taped the trigger to full throttle, so the saw would not stop. I taped the cylindrical blade-guard open until the aggressive silver-colored blade became fully exposed. Its viciously sharp teeth were blinding to my distorted retinas.

I pushed the furiously red-hot coals in the fireplace to the left side of the fire pit. The living room was dimly lit, but I could clearly see the power outlet for the protruding plug of my circular saw. I plugged the saw into the power outlet and the blade roared ravenously with a high-pitched scream. *My heart raced with anticipation and in the late night hours of a bitterly cold Christmas Eve, 2001, my mental illness finally consumed me.*

I. First Signs

The Journey Begins

My mother and father both graduated from New Mexico State University in Las Cruces. My father had studied mechanical engineering there. The grades I earned during my freshman year at the University of New Mexico were not impressive. I therefore decided to follow in my father's footsteps, hoping to succeed as he had. My father excelled in his pursuits of both mechanical engineering and Reserve Officer Training Corp (ROTC) training. My experience proved to be much different. I was nineteen years of age when I transferred from the University of New Mexico to the New Mexico State University. My course load was eighteen credit hours during the fall semester of 1989, which included calculus, physics and chemistry. After just one month, I was failing my course work miserably.

My efforts in ROTC during that semester were not progressing well either. I became uncontrollably agitated during an evening ROTC function when I witnessed my superior officer kissing the female cadet I was romantically pursuing. My superior officer tried to calm me, but I was inconsolably intoxicated. I quickly fled from the party, and damaged my 1969 VW Bug after colliding with a curb, whilst recklessly travelling back to my campus dorm room. I failed my ROTC college military entrance exam the next day. My ROTC commander harshly reprimanded me for my conduct at the party. I became extremely disappointed in myself, due to the fact I could not accomplish what my father had conquered. I experienced my first bout with depression at the age of nineteen.

However, my depression was quickly resolved with an ensuing period of hypomania. I abandoned all rational thought before attempting to pass my mid-term examinations. I decided to sell my VW, in order to leave all of my failings far behind. I spent the money on a one-way airline ticket to London, England. My mind was racing with grandiose images of a bright future in Europe. I owned no credit cards, and had only a few hundred dollars in my pocket, but prepared myself for an overseas adventure. I wrote a letter to my parents, Robert and Kathryn, before departing explaining my failing status, at New Mexico State University, and plans for Europe. My father, a colonel in the United States Air Force, was stationed at Madill Air Force Base in Tampa at the time.

On the morning of my flight, I decided it was crucial for me to dress in the proper attire for Europe. I wore my favorite pair of torn blue jeans and a tight black t-shirt. My ears were pierced, and safety pins hung from the many holes, which I had created myself. I felt I was going blend in with the punk-rock culture of England. I planned to drink beer and seek employment at a lively London pub upon my arrival. I truly believed my new life, full of endless possibilities was about to begin.

My flight left El Paso, Texas that afternoon. I flew to New York and then London. I casually walked through the Gatwick airport and handed my passport to the customs officer, who asked me the purpose of my visit. I was ignorant, but honest as I told him of my plans and he replied "Follow me." I was escorted to an inner office where another agent awaited me. She was a very rigid English woman. I loved the sound of her British accent, but not the words that exited her mouth.

The female customs agent stated the United Kingdom government was unable to grant me admission into the country, since I had no returning flight to the United States. Further, she said, with crisp diction, I owned no credit cards and had very little cash. The agent then explained there was a flight returning to the United States in four hours and I would "most assured" be on it. Finally, she told me "morally" I should pay for my ticket home. She was unaware I was hanging on by a thread and morals were the last attribute of which I possessed.

An airport security officer escorted me to a small green room until the time came for my departure back to the United States. The room was filled with some very interesting characters, which were being ejected from the country as well. I knew my parents had not yet received my letter, so I proceeded to remove a more presentable set of clothing from my luggage. I would have to live with them in Tampa, since I had already dropped all of my courses at New Mexico State University.

The security agent arrived to escort me to my departing flight's gateway after a short time had elapsed. He stayed with me until I boarded the plane. The 747 airliner soon taxied to the runway and took flight. I stared through the plane's small window with regret as we left England's airspace. I suffered from a great amount of remorse and shame as depression began to overwhelm my mind during the long flight. I was certain my parents would be shocked by my erratic behavior, and very disappointed in me as their son.

I landed in Atlanta, Georgia eight hours later. I had very little money and lacked the ability to purchase an airline ticket to Tampa. I did not know what to tell my parents. I found a public pay phone and hesitantly dialed my parent's phone number. My father answered the phone, heard my voice, and was as jovial as ever. He asked me how things were at New Mexico State University. I had not been telling him that I had failed my courses. I was in tears as I explained to my father I was in Atlanta, and needed an airline ticket to Tampa. He was confused as to why I was not in Las Cruces, New Mexico. I told him I could not explain why over the phone. My parents purchased the ticket for me without hesitation and I flew to Tampa a few hours later. I decided to tell my mother and father the truth once in their presence.

My parents were at the Tampa airport when I arrived. They wore smiles of bewilderment on their faces. However, it was a genuine greeting and good to see. I needed to feel welcomed by them. We headed to their home where I explained the whole ordeal in detail. My father and mother were very concerned, regarding my irrational thought process. My parents were confused and disappointed, but not angry. I decided not to divulge my recent depression to them, so they suspected nothing of my mood swings. I myself was unaware of the severity of my mental state. I had never heard of the terms hypomania, bi-polar, or knew of the effects which depression could or would have upon my life.

I was deeply depressed, regarding my failed studies and trip to London. My parents requested I seek employment in Tampa, so I spent the remainder of the fall months working as a banquet server. The job was not challenging and I found myself becoming restless. The banquet manager asked me if I had ever tended a bar on New Year's Eve of 1989. I responded I had not, but would try. I became incredibly drunk on white wine while bartending. I threw-up an hour later, was fired, and shattered the glass door to my parent's condominium entrance. My parents questioned if I had destroyed the door the next morning. I looked them in the eye and told them I had not. I lied further and said I quit my job. I was only sinking deeper, but attempted to displace the negative occurrences of the past four months from my mind.

My father requested I return to the University of New Mexico for the spring semester. I flew to Albuquerque on January 14th 1990. I went back to college with a new determination to succeed, and the complete ability to suppress my difficult memories of the past. I met with a college advisor upon my re-admission to the university and declared political science (International Politics) to be my major course of study.

I declared my minor in the fall of 1990. I desired to study the German language. My family had lived in Hahn, Germany when I was a child and I became intrigued by the German culture. I liked the language due to its guttural pronunciation and the fact it sounded tough. I also began to learn a great deal more about the English language, which I failed to discover during my former years of public education.

Les Miserables

My grades at University of New Mexico began to improve, as I grew more motivated to gain pride within myself, and earn my parent's respect. My college degree progressed well and I experienced a respite from drastic moods swings. I lived in the campus dormitories during the spring semester of my junior year. My small room was adjacent to another room during that semester. The layout was called a suite. My suitemate would often ask me if I wanted to be an usher for any of the upcoming theatrical shows at our campus' Popejoy hall. I usually responded to my suitemate's query I was not interested. However, I finally agreed to usher for one of the shows before the semester's end.

I walked from my dormitory room to Popejoy hall, where my level of interest in the experience increased as I entered the 2,000-seat theatre. The large stage, red-velvet covered seats, and orchestra pit were all beautifully compelling to me. I grew very curious as to what might occur on stage. I assisted patrons in finding their correct seat for an hour when the theater's bright lights began to dim. The show was sold-out, so I sat on the stairs of the mezzanine. Once the theater was completely dark, the music began.

I had not yet experienced a sense of awe for anything at that point in my young life. Speechless was not a term my limited vocabulary consisted of. *Les Miserables* changed everything. My eyes never left the stage during the lengthy show. My ears never heard such intensity. I had never been so emotionally moved. The singers were phenomenal and the dramatic story was truly compelling. The staging was unbelievable. I was speechless and in awe as I viewed something incredible to me. My mind began to race. I did not desire for it to end and needed more. I was not satisfied with simply watching the amazing spectacle… I wanted to be in it.

I walked to a local record shop the next day and purchased the London cast tape-recording of *Les Miserables*. I brazenly walked back to my dorm room, where I played the soundtrack on my stereo and was immediately transported back to the theatre. I listened to *Les Miserables* repeatedly, hour upon hour. I naturally began to sing along as I became more familiar with the music. I sang under my breath at first, but started to sing louder as I gained a greater knowledge of the songs. I sang loudly until I heard something foreign to me. I was creating the voice of a singer.

I gained confidence, vocally, with every repetition of *Les Miserables* and started to play only my favorite tunes. These consisted of Javer's epic musical pieces. Javer was a dark character and his part was quite comfortable for my voice. I discovered my vocal quality to be similar with that of the performer's, thus began my tutelage from him. I also started to be inspired by Javert's ominous presence, whilst singing along. I sang passionately.

I vocalized every day. Eventually, I began to produce a decent singing voice. Vocal guidance was necessary for me, however. It was mid-way through the semester, so I was not able to start voice lessons until the next fall. I mimicked the singers on the soundtrack for months. I concluded they were the best and decided to further learn from them. My mind was racing and I became extremely energized, due to my newfound passion for singing.

I enrolled in classical vocal training prior to the fall semester of 1991 and changed my minor course of study from German to Music (vocal performance). I met with my voice professor during the first week of classes. Robert Jones was a tall man, with a medium build. He asked me about myself and the reasons I wanted to sing. I told him of my experience at *Les Miserables*. Mr. Jones asked me to sing something from the musical. I roared out a selection from the show without hesitation or accompaniment. Robert told me he was happy to have me as a student, since he would not have to force the sound from me. He went on to say a great amount of refinement would be necessary.

Mr. Jones helped me to use my powerful voice effectively. I had only just begun my vocal training, but planned to pursue a career in the performing arts. My parents became aware of my passion for musicals. My father was concerned I desired to perform professionally. My mother was supportive of the decision. I occasionally sang for them after my encounter with *Les Miserables,* and they both agreed I had a certain amount of talent. My ego began to inflate with every passing day while singing in my dorm room. I projected upon becoming the greatest singer in the world.

However, my enthusiasm for classical vocal training and opera studio soon diminished after beginning the semester. I was studying and singing songs in Italian and the diction of the language became difficult for me. My professors and I never seemed to be working on my voice. We spent most of our time on the pronunciation of the Italian language. I became frustrated, due to my craving to sing epic pieces of music in English. I thus explored other avenues for my vocal desires.

I acquired a class schedule for the upcoming spring semester and researched courses available to students in the theater program. One such course was Musical Theater Workshop. It concentrated on learning how to audition for the musical theater. I procured the name of the professor who was instructing the class and visited his office as soon as I was able. He explained I had to audition, to be enrolled in the course. I auditioned a week later, singing *Stars* from *Les Miserables*. The professor thanked me for my performance and I departed with great anticipation of becoming a student in the class.

My mind began to race from the moment I left the audition. The emotions I experienced afterward were intense. I believed my audition had gone incredibly well and believed the professor must have been extremely impressed with my vocal abilities. However, after several hours of such self-aggrandizing I began to think of what I should have done differently. My mind soon after lost its momentum and I started to judge myself harshly.

The musical theater professor called the next day and told me classes were to begin on the following Tuesday. I was elated to be accepted into the course and became rejuvenated in my desire to excel during my voice lessons with Mr. Jones. My vocal quality was improving. Robert trained my voice well. He taught me about the many aspects of singing and how to use my voice in a healthy manner. Mr. Jones desired for me to have a long career as a performer. He and I both knew I could not preserve my voice while singing at the volume I was without proper training.

I learned the subtleties of my voice and started to produce a healthier sound. Robert and I concentrated on the vocal chords, breathing techniques, and dynamics. I learned about the muscles below the diaphragm and how to use them. Mr. Jones instructed breath control, positioning of the body, space, tension, the upper palate, and projection. He was a great instructor, very practical, and wonderful to work with.

II. Beginning of the End

Sweeney Todd

The musical theater course taught me the tools for performing a song. I learned how to stand, walk, and live every nuance of the characters I was portraying. I believed my weekly performances were well received by the professor and fellow classmates. However, during one of our class sessions a female student asked me where I was from. I told her I had lived in many places. She commented my singing voice sounded as if I was from England. The other classmates agreed with her.

I was upset by the young woman's criticism. I truly believed my talents were superior to all others and despised her for having any comment, other than praise, to advance in my direction. My anger subsided as I remembered I had initially learned how to sing by listening to the London cast recording of *Les Miserables*. I mimicked their voices and was singing with English vowels. The instructor, along with Mr. Jones led me to find my own voice, regarding singing and accents.

Most of my class sessions in the musical theater course were filled with singing passionless tunes, filled with sentiments of love and endless devotion. I gave up all hope of there being another dark and deeply moving musical similar to *Les Miserables*. My dissatisfaction was quelled before the semester ended when a classmate played a video that stirred me. The video cassette filled the television with an image of two strangely costumed characters. They were performing a piece called *A Little Priest* from the musical *Sweeney Todd*. I was disturbed and overwhelmed by its subject matter. Misses Lovett and Sweeney Todd were singing a song about meat pies containing human flesh. I needed to know more about the musical only moments after viewing the short video excerpt.

I acquired the London Cast recording of *Sweeney Todd* the next morning. I began playing *Sweeney Todd* on my car stereo that afternoon, while driving to my grandparent's cabin in the mountains of Northern New Mexico. I soon realized why it was touted as a "Musical thriller." I could see the story unfold before my eyes. Steven Sondheim had created a home for me. I imagined a place full of intrigue, where love and hate were in abundance.

I stopped at a secluded area before reaching the cabin, in order to listen intently to the last fifteen minutes of *Sweeney Todd*. My mind raced as my ears-drums partook of every descriptive lyric. It was the most incredible conclusion to any story I had ever known. I was inspired by the masterpiece and quickly drove to the cabin, where a cassette player and two very loud speakers awaited me.

I became more and more obsessed with *Sweeney Todd* with every passing day. I found the singing to be rich and often heavy. The part of Sweeney Todd was a powerful role. I discovered Sweeney's singing range to be very similar with my own. Further, I began to encompass and project the character of Sweeney Todd in my daily life. He was a brutal menace to society. Sweeney Todd's wit was as sharp as his deadly straight razor.

Sweeney's musical numbers were epic. I understood his anger and subsequent rage. I wanted to be as hateful as he, regarding the outside world. I became a veritable Jekyll and Hyde. I laughed, then cried, and finally raged at the injustices of humanity while listening to the soundtrack repeatedly. My mood swings became intense… Changing daily, if not hourly.

I desired a symbol of my passion for the darkness within my life, after just a month since acquiring the soundtrack, so I visited a tattoo parlor in Albuquerque. I had the name of the musical tattooed down my back. The tattoo read "Sweeney Todd" in black Roman type lettering. It was my first tattoo. The needle initially caused pain as it pierced my skin. I found I really enjoyed the pain as the artist continued for two hours. I became extremely exhilarated and energized during the session. It was my first experience with the fascination and need for self-inflicted scars.

A month later, I auditioned for the Albuquerque Civic Light Opera Association's production of *Once Upon a Mattress*. I was cast as Sir Studley. I was in the chorus. There was no pay, only the chance to gain theatrical experience. I did the best I could with the depth of my part. I was not satisfied with the size of my role and the simplicity of the character. The character, which encompassed me when off-stage, was growing progressively darker.

However, I made a good impression during rehearsals and the run of the show. I was able to project and maintain a professional demeanor when in the company of my fellow cast members. Theater friends and I went to parties together. I felt my good reputation would eventually pay-off. It did not long after completing my debut role on stage.

I was cast as Rooster in the Albuquerque Little Theater's production of *Annie*. I loved the villainous character of Rooster. Most of the shows were sold-out and I was told that my portrayal of Rooster was very good. My ego began to inflate even further. I believed I was the most talented and interesting actor in the production. My reputation started to gain attention, negatively.

Soon after performances of Annie began, I discovered the Albuquerque Civic Light Opera Association was to perform *Sweeney Todd* the following year at Popejoy hall. My mind raced with anticipation to play the title role in the large and beautiful theater. My mood-swings began to gain momentum, in frequency, and intensity.

I started to mark my territory by singing Sweeney's songs from *Sweeney Todd* while applying make-up before performances of *Annie*. There was a singer in the dressing room next to mine who was hoping to be cast in the role of Sweeney Todd. He was older and fit the part, because of his age. I did not think he possessed the voice to perform the role, however. Sweeney was demanding of a great singer and I believed my abilities far outweighed the other man's. In addition, he lacked my passion for the show and its lead character. Simply stated, he was not obsessed with *Sweeney Todd*.

The Albuquerque Civic Light Opera Association held auditions for *Sweeney Todd* during my last semester at the University of New Mexico. I auditioned by singing *Epiphany* from the show. It was a performance to remember. *Epiphany* projects Sweeney's declaration of vengeance upon all of humanity as retribution for the pain he has suffered. It was an intense audition. Todd Lawson LaTourrette was not singing the dark tune. I truly transformed into Sweeney Todd.

I was granted a callback for the part of Sweeney Todd. The other man who fit the age range for the role was also given a callback. The director had me sing *Joanna*. During *Joanna*,

Sweeney sings about the loss of his daughter's presence and love, while slitting the throats of un-suspecting customers with a straight razor. I felt I devoured the part. I had never slit a throat before, but projected I understood the emotion necessary for such a vengeful act. I drove home to Santa Fe after the callback. My mind began to race during the drive. I believed my performance had been exceptional, and subsequently earned the part of Sweeney Todd.

Time passed slowly as I waited for a phone call from the director. He called after several hours and what he told me was devastating. The director cast me as Anthony. The other man was to be Sweeney Todd. My heart sank. I believed my acting and singing to be flawless. The director told me he thought I was too young to play the role of Sweeney. His honesty and my attempt to understand did not prevent me from sinking deeply into despair, however.

Anthony was the young love interest of Sweeney Todd's long lost daughter Joanna. I was typecast. My face was youthful and I had blonde hair. I decided to throw myself into the role, however. I desired to portray the best Anthony anyone ever witnessed. I rehearsed my songs and lines daily. The musical takes place in London. I already knew how to sing with an English accent, so I planned to perform it well.

However, I was unable to transgress the fact I had not been cast as Sweeney Todd. I was extremely jealous, which often translated as anger. My obsession with *Sweeney Todd* was ceaseless. I nearly dropped my course of study at the University of New Mexico that semester. Depression was crashing upon me in an insurmountable scale. I returned to the tattoo artist with the desire for a much-needed jolt of exhilaration. He added the words

"The Demon Barber of Fleet Street" under "Sweeney Todd." The tattoo was finished with a slash and solitary drip of blood falling from its edge.

I suffered from incredible mood swings during the run of *Sweeney Todd*. Everyone was aware of my erratic behavior and my relationships were affected. I truly did not care what others thought of me, however. I wanted to be Sweeney Todd and watching someone else, someone less qualified perform the role, was extremely difficult for me. I was overly energetic while on stage and depressed when not.

Performances of *Sweeney Todd* finished in December of 1993. I graduated from the University of New Mexico that same month and decided to make musical theater my career. I had found a place where my mood-swings could easily be disguised as effective acting. I truly discovered the arts were a place where I would be tolerated.

Summer Stock

I stepped outside of myself, and Todd ceased to exist throughout my young career performing in the community theater of Albuquerque. I submersed myself into every role. I had quickly become a method actor. Further, my motivation and desire was to become someone else. I was no longer content with playing the role of Todd Lawson La Tourrette. Todd had flaws and plenty of baggage. I believed the characters I portrayed possessed more interesting attributes than my own. They were confident, funny, deep, dark, and impassioned by life. I had a talent for portraying and pretending I too possessed these qualities.

I focused all of my efforts on becoming a professional actor after graduating in December of 1993. I knew community theatre would never satisfy the amount of stimulation I required. Therefore, my grandmother gave me her old car, in order for me to travel east that January. I decided to drive from Virginia to New York City for auditions, so I joined my brother Scott on the east coast.

My first audition was a cattle call in Manhattan. I performed for several regional theaters that held one audition together. I performed *The Masochism Tango* by Tom Lehrer and Sam Byck's monologue from the musical *Assassins*. I sang and acted the disturbing characters passionately during the audition. I only received one callback, however. It was for a theater in Wisconsin. I sang a piece from Yeston and Kopit's musical *Phantom* at my callback. It was a powerful song. I was not familiar with it, but reveled in the possibility I might play the title role. The man thanked me and I returned to Virginia the next day.

My time on the east coast was short. I drove to New York City for several auditions, but only received the one callback. My grandiosity fleeted and my moods darkened daily with thoughts of professional inadequacy. The director of the theater in Wisconsin called me a few weeks after my initial audition. He wanted to hire me for their 1993 summer season. I agreed to his offer without hesitation. I was not concerned with the monetary amount of my contract. I was simply thrilled to begin my career in the art of acting.

Summer-stock in Wisconsin was my first professional acting job. My parents were proud of my ability to secure employment as a performer. My mind was racing with a newly revitalized sense of grandiosity while driving to Wisconsin. Thoughts of a brilliant future encompassed me. However, I found the experience to be very different from my initial expectations. I worked night and day for a small salary. We did not perform *Jekyll and Hyde*, but I certainly acted as if we were.

I performed the title role in *Phantom* and Lt. Cable in *South Pacific*. I also acted in *Noises Off* and *Arsenic and Old Lace*. We began the summer season with *Phantom*. The cast started performances of the show and we then rehearsed *South Pacific*. When *South Pacific* was ready, we added it to the mix. The other shows followed in the same manner. Our cast performed a different show every night of the week.

I was honored to play the lead role in *Phantom* and felt my performances were exceptional. My ego inflated to a degree from which there was no return. My voice was powerful and filled with dark tones. I absorbed every evil nuance of the character and portrayed them convincingly. I truly transformed into the Phantom with the very same passion I had for Sweeney Todd. Once again, I believed the other cast members possessed little talent. I performed each role as if no one else existed on stage with me.

My mood swings played a powerful role in my life, on-stage and off, during the three months in Wisconsin. The moods I was experiencing were detrimental to my ability for rational thought and behavior. The entire cast lived together, so they all witnessed every change in mood that I experienced. No one could live or work with me. I made friends when energized and lost them when deeply depressed. I could not understand why the owner did not fire me. My only conclusion was he needed my talent… whatever the cost.

I left Wisconsin in September and quickly suppressed all of the negative memories of my transgressions. I convinced myself I had done well, while blissfully ignorant of my reality. I hurt people with my actions and reactions, but had no knowledge of it. I hated my life one minute and believed I was a superstar the next. I could not focus on other people's needs. Everyone else's hopes and dreams did not cross my mind. My career continued to progress however, due to my talent alone. Talent, while performing, was my only tangible contribution to the world at that point in my young life.

III. Newly Acquired Skills and Patterns

Carpentry

I returned to Santa Fe in September of 1993. My mother soon after told me about a style of furniture which she had discovered in a local shop. She described the style to me, so I accompanied her to the furniture store where we looked at the style. The furniture was beautiful. Long, straight sticks were included into the design. My mother further explained her desire for the style in my parent's master bedroom windows. I was confident I could build her two stylish shutters before we departed the store. My mother was not as convinced. I wanted to prove to myself I was capable, even though I had no previous carpentry experience or abilities.

Undaunted, I immediately drove to the nearest hardware store. I purchased a skill-saw and chuck-less drill. I also procured wood, screws, nails, sandpaper, brushes, and wood stain. The cost was over seven-hundred dollars, which I charged to my credit card. I realized I needed a bundle of long sticks after returning home. There was a solitary tree on the property next to my parent's home that would satisfy the required materials. I spent hours cutting the gray colored branches from its trunk. I then measured the space where my mother desired her shutters to hang and proceeded to the garage.

I started to create the shutters late into the evening. I worked throughout the night in my parent's garage. I cut one inch by four inch by eight feet fine finish pine boards to the necessary specifications I decided upon. I ripped the wood into the given lengths without hesitation. I assembled two-thirds of the frame and stained them.

I cut the sticks to fit inside the frames at a diagonal angle. I secured the sticks to the inside of the frame with small nails. The sticks where nailed into place one by one. The inside of the frame was one-inch narrower than the exterior of the frame, so the nails were not visible. I was then ready to place the back exterior boards onto the frame. My mind was racing and my body could barely keep up with its pace.

I marveled at my creation once I was finished. I believed it was possible, and completed the project. It took me seven hours from start to finish. I entered the house with my mother's new stylish shutters the next morning. My father and I hung the shutters which fitted perfectly. My parents were amazed and my mother was very thankful. They were honored to have my first piece of carpentry in their bedroom. However, my parents were concerned for me as they witnessed my greatly elevated energy level while building the shutters.

I started working as a singing waiter in Santa Fe after completing the addition to my parent's home. The restaurant accommodated sixty guests and was very cozy. The other singers and I performed our songs in a cabaret style venue. Singing in such a setting was intoxicating. The guests enjoyed my performances and were always full of compliments. Their praise was welcome, and truly stroked my already massive performing ego.

I performed musical theater pieces during the nightly shows at the restaurant. I worked hard to possess my powerful voice, but never pursued opera. The language barrier of most operas did not appeal to me. I desired for the audience to be in the moment with me while performing. I wished for them to experience, first hand, every ounce of darkness within my performances. I wanted to create tension with my intensity. The joy I sang about caused them to be joyous. The audience experienced the array of every emotion that I did. I believed I was very effective after realizing this to be the actor's purpose.

I sang Tom Lehrer's *The Masochism Tango* every night. I was extremely animated when performing the song. The guests loved my wild performance of it. My energy level was as massive as my over-confident stage personality. I occasionally entertained older guests, for whom I added many a bizarre accentuation to the masochistic side of myself. I was larger than life itself while performing.

My darker side filled the night as well. I often performed *Transformation* from the musical *Jekyll and Hyde*. I began the song with the beautiful soft tones of Jekyll. I turned into Hyde as the song progressed. My voice darkened, along with my personality. My face and body convulsed as I experienced the rage within the character and myself. I was truly releasing the pain of my own life in the healthiest manner I knew of… on stage. Exhaustion would always set-in after every performance of *Transformation*. I smiled to the guests as they applauded my performance, but only desired solitude. I was truly transforming my own passion for life into the desire for its destruction nightly.

Self-medicating

I resided with my parents during that period of my life. My family did not know about my troubles in Wisconsin. Self-preservation caused me to believe the difficulties I experienced there were merely due to the circumstances. My mother and father were pleased I was pursuing my goal of an acting career. They were even proud of my few accomplishments. I was singing and making money because of my talents.

I received much praise from our guests at the restaurant in Santa Fe. The other singers had talent as well, but I always felt they were inferior to me. My inflated ego caused me to project I was the best. I always believed myself to be flawless while performing. In fact, I truly thought I was the greatest singer in the world.

I judged the other singers on their talent alone and not on their individual qualities. My colleagues were wonderful people. They were good friends to me. I enjoyed their company a great deal. I was extremely energized, but they seemed to like this about me. I was the crazy person who drank a bit too much after work, and told wildly inappropriate stories. However, the other singers and I never spent much time together outside of work. I was living with my parents and considered them my only friends. In reality, my parents were the only people who would, or could, tolerate my mood swings.

I became restless in Santa Fe after only a few months, so I made a phone call to an actress from my prior Wisconsin summer-stock job. She was living in Chicago, Illinois at the time and we talked at length. Jill explained she had recently finished a contract performing on a cruise liner. I asked her the name of the production company she worked for, and Jill told me Norwegian Cruise Lines would soon be auditioning in Chicago. This information aroused my curiosity. I focused my efforts on gaining an audition after she told me what the contract's salary was for a singer. I was determined to succeed before boarding the airplane to Chicago, Illinois.

Jill was at the airport when I arrived. The next morning we went to the audition space, where I prepared myself for the audition. I performed *Empty Chairs at Empty Tables* from *Les Miserables*. I was absolutely brimming with confidence and believed the director had no other choice than to hire me. I flew back to Santa Fe the next day and waited for a call from the production company. The phone did not ring as soon as I hoped for.

My desire to work at the restaurant expired soon after my audition in Chicago. I grew weary of singing the same songs every night, so resigned and began working as a security guard at a local nightclub. I expected nothing gratifying to come from the position, and was only distracting myself while waiting to hear back from Norwegian Cruise Lines. My first night as a bouncer was interesting when I realized it was a gay bar. This fact affected me in no way negatively. I was exhilarated by the attention I received.

I decided to dance on the bar after work one evening. The owner then asked me if I wanted to dance professionally for the club. I was somewhat muscular, due to my efforts at a local gym, so I told her I would love to. I jumped on stage in front of the crowd and removed my shirt during my first night as a striptease dancer. The crowd was dancing as well and did not give me the amount of attention I was craving. Thus, I decided to get more creative and risqué the following night.

I purchased a few interesting and possibly sexy outfits before my next shift. In addition, I acquired some rave goggles at a local shop. I arrived at the club later that evening prepared to make more of a lively impression. I found my costumes did not stay on for very long and enjoyed the exhilaration it caused. Most people feel better about themselves when they help an elderly woman cross the street. I felt bliss when my ego was being vastly inflated. However, my days of striptease dancing in Santa Fe came to a brief conclusion when the Norwegian Cruise Line production company called with a contract.

I was cast as a lead singer on the *S.S. Norway* in November of 1995. It was the flagship for Norwegian Cruise Lines. I flew to Ft. Lauderdale, Florida and began the rehearsal process. My moods were stable for the beginning of my contract. I made friends with most everyone while in rehearsals. I was full of energy and well received. A married couple and I spent much of our downtime together. They were both dancers. The woman thought I was extremely talented and often told me so. The high of all highs always ensued after such praise.

The company of performers was driven to Miami after the rehearsal period ended and we boarded the *S.S. Norway*. I settled into my single cabin for an hour and then walked throughout the ship. It was enormous. I asked another employee were I could find the crew bar while gazing upon the vast ocean surrounding me. He pointed me toward the back of the ship. I found the bar with ease, because of the raucous noise exuding from within. I wanted to celebrate my success and became intoxicated during the process.

The other cast members soon joined me in the crew bar. There were many other crewmembers in the bar as well. Employees from the casino, spa, and dining rooms filled the small tavern. I was the new person and very outgoing. Making friends fast was my style, (this characteristic was formed while the son of a military man). I made a big impression during my first night on the ship. My over-bearing personality quickly caused the other crewmembers to become weary of me, however. This fact did not keep me from getting drunk and even more so flamboyant.

Our cast began rehearsals on stage the next morning. I was extremely hung-over. The *S.S. Norway* was the largest cruise liner on the seas at the time, so the captain decided to steer through a hurricane in the Gulf of Mexico that week. The ship tossed and turned, up then down. There was a bathroom off-stage and I made good use of it. I went on stage, sang for a minute, and then ran into the bathroom to vomit. This occurred for the entire six-hour rehearsal period.

I was one of two male vocalists in the shows. The cast performed a Broadway style show, a Vegas style show, and *Will Rogers Follies*. Each show was fifty minutes in length. We did two shows per night. I worked a total of fourteen hours per week. This fact gave me a plethora of opportunities to drink alcohol. I didn't sun bathe too often, and never had the energy to work out in the gym. I drank beer instead

My visits to the crew bar began as a social outlet. I tried to make friends, but only made acquaintances. Cast and crew would tolerate me for an hour and then leave. My mood-swings began to include depression once again. I remained highly energized on stage, but became deeply depressed when not. My heavy consumption of alcohol did not assist with my waning mental health, or relationships with others.

There was a small refrigerator in my cabin room that cooled twelve beers. I purchased beer by the case. There were never less than five cases of bottled brew stacked in the corner of my room at one time. I was deeply depressed and self-medicating with alcohol. I lived this way for months, drinking a twelve pack or more a day. I became trapped in my own vicious cycle, within which alcohol only intensified and perpetuated my feelings of depression.

However, my performances kept me exhilarated. That old feeling of euphoria existed while singing and dancing. I had seven costume changes during the shows. I sang for five minutes and then would exit the stage. I then rushed back to the stage after quickly changing. The female dancers had even more costume changes. They wore large headdresses and tight sequin costumes. The shows were larger than life and so was I.

I injured my left foot during a show not long after my contract began. It swelled immediately. The ship's doctor could not decide whether it was a sprain or actually broken. He took x-rays, but they were inconclusive. The *S.S. Norway* docked in Miami the next week, where a Florida physician concluded I had broken a bone in my foot. Thus, I returned to Santa Fe for six weeks of recovery.

I managed to completely forget why I had been experiencing depression while on vacation in the Southwest. My mind was thinking more clearly, due to the lack of alcohol I was drinking daily on the ship. I was resolute in making a good impression on my old cast mates when I returned to fulfill my contract. They welcomed me back and were happy to see me. It was not a week's time before I was drinking heavily and deeply depressed again.

I ate my meals in the cast and crew dining room during the beginning of my contract. My meals consisted of peanut butter sandwiches, cereal, and pasta noodles with soy sauce. Familiar faces would simply exchange "hi" and "goodbye" with me. I met a new cast member who found me interesting three months before my contract ended. She had not yet experienced all that was Todd. My mood swings ended the relationship after only a month and I was once again alone.

I soon began to eat my meals in the officer dining room, because of its selection of better breakfast cereals. I always ate alone, but did become friendly with the custodian who worked there. The man was quiet and nice to me. He lifted my feelings of depression by simply talking with me and smiling at something I said. During one of our cruises, he wrote a suicide note and leapt from the back of the ship. No one witnessed his final act and he was never found. Suicide had made an impact upon my life for the first time and became a possible solution for an alternative to life's trials and tribulations.

IV. Self-destructive

Cutting

My contract ended after nine months on the *S.S. Norway*. I had
made acquaintances, but no true friends. I became more aware of
the feelings I was experiencing on the ship upon my return to
Santa Fe. Depression had followed me home. My mother talked
with me at length and she recommended I visit a psychiatrist. I
had a great amount of respect for my mother's opinion, but felt
there was something negative about seeking the advice of a
psychiatrist. I did not want to need help. I believed I would be
losing a certain amount of power over my own life. I went to see
the psychiatrist regardless of my hesitation to do so.

The psychiatrist asked me about myself. I was candid and
told him about my past difficulties. I believed my energized highs
to be part of my best attributes, so decided not to include the
details of such to him. The psychiatrist told me I was not alone.
He explained medications would help with my depression. He
also recommended therapy. I did not want to hear what he
advised. The last thing I wanted to do was take a hand-full of pills.
I feared friends and colleagues would judge me, due to my
necessity for assistance. I was not a willing patient, but took the
antidepressant prescription from his outreaching hand.

I needed relief from the depression I was experiencing, even
if it meant taking medications. I told my parents about the

doctor's suggestions on my way to the local drug store. My parents were both relieved I had seen the doctor and sought his assistance. They were amazed I was willing to take the medication. The pharmacy filled my prescription and we returned home.

The first dose was difficult for me to take. I took my medication later that evening and went to sleep. My desire for the medication to have an immediate positive effect was hopeful, but not practical. I was still deeply depressed. My mother and I were at the same grocery store, as the psychiatrist not long after my initial appointment. He greeted me in a friendly manner and asked how I was feeling. I answered honestly that I was experiencing no relief. The doctor told me to allow for more time. He then told my mother the store was giving away free paring knives, and with that information, my psychiatrist departed.

My mother and I entered the grocery store in order to shop. Mom acquired the free knife and we continued with our shopping. I inquired to see the paring knife once we had arrived home. My mother thought nothing of my request and showed it to me. I was living at home and soon retired to bed. My mother went to sleep shortly thereafter. My father was on a business trip in Atlanta, Georgia.

I emerged from my room later that evening with a single-minded purpose. I found the paring knife in the kitchen utensil drawer. I walked to the downstairs bathroom and locked the door behind me. I proceeded to cut my entire body with the knife. I started with my arms. The cuts were not very deep. However, I experienced a temporary relief from my depression as I cut. I was energized by the cutting and discovered a truly delusional avenue to my desired heightened state of mind.

I unlocked the door to the bathroom and called upstairs to my mother. I wanted her to witness what I had done. I was becoming ever more delusional, but exhilarated by my self-destructive act. My mother walked down the stairs to the bathroom and cried-out with fear. I immediately began to feel remorse for my behavior. The reality of my mother's reaction caused my insanity to cease.

My mother became angry with me once her initial shock subsided. She asked me why I had cut myself. I looked into her eyes, but could not think of an answer. My mother had a great amount of concern for my wellbeing and took the knife from my hand. She then told me to get into the bathtub. I filled the tub, and felt the pain of the cuts for the first time as the warm water encompassed my body. My mother told me to clean the wounds with soap. The pain increased as I washed my entire body.

I was exhausted after bathing and passed-out in bed. My mother did not sleep that night. She watched over me until morning. I awoke with a sense of dread as the rising sun was shedding its streams of golden light into my bedroom. I realized what I had done to my mother's state of mind and asked for her forgiveness. I was not concerned for myself. My mother insisted I see my psychiatrist that afternoon. I reluctantly agreed.

I told the psychiatrist what had occurred. He recommended more medications. I once again took his advice and prescription. My prescription was filled and I returned home to find my father who was awaiting my arrival. He had left his business trip early in order to support my mother and me. I feared he would be angry, regarding my self-destructive behavior, but found he showed a great amount of concern instead.

We talked about my actions for days. I took my medications as prescribed and played the part of a good patient. I stopped taking my medications a week later after healing both body and mind. I was in a heightened state of exhilaration, because of the cutting, and that is where I desired to be. I went on with my life as if nothing had happened.

Will the Sun come out?

I was undaunted by my experience of cutting and still desired to pursue an acting career. I had saved enough money from my contract on the *S.S. Norway* to make another effort at New York City. I drove east in September of 1995. My newly re-painted car made quite an impression in Manhattan. I spray painted my car black and white the week before I departed from Santa Fe. It looked very much like a police cruiser. I was completely energized and New York City proved to be the perfect place for my altered state of mind.

I moved into a two bedroom and one bath apartment on the upper west side. My rent was five hundred dollars a month. I had saved more than $3,000 during my contract on the ship, so I lived comfortably without having to work. My roommate was an aspiring actor as well. She and I did not spend a great amount of time together, but got along well enough.

My first auditions in New York were difficult. I had learned to sing a song in its entirety during my education in college. The auditions in New York City were limited to sixteen bars of music. I did not have any songs that lent themselves to this length. Further, I believed my talent could not be fully understood with just sixteen bars. I received only one callback from my many auditions during September and October.

In late October, I discovered an audition notice for the east coast tour of *Annie* while reading a New York actor's trade paper. My heart pounded heavily within my chest as I read the breakdown. I believed I would have a good chance of getting a part, since I had already played the role of Rooster with the Albuquerque Little Theater. The tour was non-equity, so I knew hundreds of singers would attend. I was one of the first actors to arrive early on the day of the audition. The piece I performed for the director was *Easy Street* from *Annie*. I wore an especially bright colored jacket and danced the original choreography while singing. He allowed me thirty-two bars and I believed my performance to be exceptional. I left the audition thinking I earned the part of Rooster.

Depression found its way back into my moods again while waiting to hear from the *Annie* director. Thus, I decided to have my "Sweeney Todd" tattoo removed. I walked to a dermatologist's office the next day, hoping the painful removal process would cause a much-needed energized state of mind. I discovered my hypothesis to be completely correct during my first visit. The pain from the laser was much more intense than that of a tattooing needle.

I experienced a high that was more invigorating than any of my past episodes. I was told to come back for a second appointment after the first tattoo removal healed. My tattoo was nearly removed three sessions later. My heart and mind raced due to the pain from each session. I always left the dermatologist's office exhilarated, and brazenly walked the lengthy distance through Central Park to my apartment. I was back on top of the world again after having gladly spent two thousand dollars for the painful removal.

I received a phone call from the director of the national tour in late November. He told me I was cast in the part of Rooster. I was ecstatic, but needed a break from New York so drove to visit my brother Scott in Virginia the next day. We celebrated my good fortune when I arrived. The holiday season was in full swing and it was nice to be with family. I was not able to spend Christmas with Scott that year, however. I drove back to Manhattan in early December, in order to start rehearsals for *Annie*.

The rehearsal space was on Broadway Avenue. I initially made friends with ease. The choreographer for the show was the wife of the director. I liked her at first and took direction well. She decided to choreograph the show differently from the original Broadway production. I was disappointed and felt her choreography to be inferior to that of the original show.

The choreographer had me drop to my knees at several points during the number *Easy Street*. I was then choreographed to stand-up and then drop to my knees again. It hurt like hell and I despised her for directing me to do so. I disliked singing and dancing the part, because of her choreography. My unfavorable attitude for the choreographer was very apparent and I made more enemies than friends as the rehearsal process progressed. I went back to the dermatologist for my final session of tattoo laser removal surgery before the tour began. I was relieved of any depression with the last dose of pain driven mood stimulation.

My parents joined me in Manhattan while I was preparing to depart with the tour. They wanted to see where I lived and how I was doing in the big city. The director of *Annie* told the cast family members were welcome to view our final rehearsal of the show. I was honored to be performing for my very loving and supportive mother and father. My parents were impressed with my singing voice and acting. My only desire was to make them proud of me.

My parents and I ate bagels and drank coffee on the rooftop of my five-story apartment building the next morning. We enjoyed the view together while looking upon the multitude of New York City's differently colored and shaped buildings. I then took my parents on a tour of Broadway Avenue. We ate pizza as we walked the sixty blocks to Times Square. We were exhausted when we arrived at forty second Street, so my parents departed to their hotel and I walked back to my apartment on one hundred and eighth street.

I met my parents downtown later that evening in order to see *Les Miserables* on Broadway. They had previously listened to the recording of *Les Miserables* many times and desired to see it performed on stage. My mother loved the music. I was excited for them to see the very musical which had flamed my desire to sing. The fact I was an employed actor living in New York City pleased me as well.

My parents left a day later and I once again felt the emptiness of being alone. I was not alone for long, as the tour promptly began. The cast gathered with their luggage at Columbus Circle early on December 23rd of 1996. We all packed into the small space when the bus arrived. It was to be our home for the next three months. I traveled the entire east coast jammed into a bus with twenty adults, two dogs, seven children, and their guardians. I soon discovered *Annie* to be a miserable show to tour with. I was living the reality of my own *Les Miserables*.

The cast was first driven to Canada where we performed for a week. It was the lengthiest stay we had during our tour. Canada was beautiful in winter. The theatre was gorgeous and a pleasure to perform in. The cast enjoyed Canada's Boxing Day enormously. I had no idea what it was about, but drank several beers with the locals anyway. I spent most of my time alone during the week in Canada. While performing I was fine. My greatest concern was for my state of mind when off-stage.

My mood swings were beyond control while on tour. My knees were destroyed because of the choreography. I exited the stage cursing the choreographer after every performance of *Easy Street*. I threw a chair in the dressing room and almost hit the show's dog Sandy on one occasion. A cast member witnessed the incident and immediately told the director. The director did nothing about the scene. I assumed he did not want to further upset me, for I was already out of control.

One of the children in the show told me her guardian had lost all of their cash money not long into the tour. I immediately became upset by their loss and proceeded to destroy my tape recorder while preparing my make-up for the performance that night. The cast did not know what had caused my anger. Many of them started to yell at me. I wanted to tell them all about the pain I was experiencing, due to the injustices of life. I became enraged by the cast's insincerity, concerning the child's loss. The director later talked to me about my actions, but did nothing. Once again, I had talent and he needed this quality in his show. I was not a narcissistic actor… I was bipolar, but simply had no knowledge of it.

I had demolished any possible friendships with my mood-swings when the *Annie* tour ended. My bouts with mania and depression were intolerable. The director never cast me in another show. However, I truly felt the tour had been a success, despite my behavior. My mind had developed an impressive self-preservation mechanism. I had disappointed many people, but only concerned myself with building upon my own career. I returned to New York and auditioned for a few more shows. Manhattan was exciting, but I grew to have a love and hate relationship for it. I left the east coast and returned to Santa Fe shortly after the tour was completed.

V. Mental Upheaval

Sky Diving

I decided to visit my brother Brad in July of 1997. Brad was living in Tampa, Florida with his wife and two children, working as a designer for an architecture firm. Brad's kids were young and being home schooled by his wife. I really enjoyed his kids. They were very different from one another, but both had Brad's same wonderful smile and sense of humor.

That year Brad purchased a family season pass for Busch Gardens, and we often went to enjoy the roller coasters. I loved the rides at the theme park, due to the rush of adrenaline they caused. However, I eventually became complacent with their predictability and soon desired a greater thrill. I wanted to do something dangerous. I looked through the phonebook for skydiving advertisements on a hot July afternoon in Florida. One in particular sounded reliable. It was a forty-five minute drive from Tampa, so I left immediately. I craved a new mind altering activity and pursued it with determination.

The drive seemed to take forever. I saw skydivers floating down with beautifully colored parachutes as I neared the venue. The sight was enthralling. I entered the parking area and walked briskly into the main office building. I was not concerned with the cost and told the clerk of my need to jump from an airplane.

The representative took my credit card, charged my account, and pointed me toward the hanger.

I looked into the sky with determination as I entered the hanger. A man met me and explained I would be skydiving with him strapped to my back. He called it a "tandem jump." He then offered me a more suitable pair of shoes for the jump, but I insisted on wearing my black cowboy boots (my boots had been on my feet for every great adventure). We entered a twin-otter aircraft after a short time. I was very eager for take-off.

There were eight other skydivers in the plane with me. They were experienced in the sport and told me I would enjoy my first jump. The twin-otter ascended and started to climb into the sky. My mind was racing with anticipation as I hoped for the thrill of a lifetime. Once we were at the drop-zone, thirteen thousand feet above the earth's surface, the other skydivers exited the aircraft, one by one.

I told my partner I was ready. He approached me and strapped our body suits together. The twin-otter did not have much headroom, so he and I moved to the open door on our knees. I looked down at the vastness of our world while kneeling at the thresh hold of the airplane and sky. The instructor asked me what I wanted to do once in the air. He explained we would have sixty seconds of free-fall before opening the parachute. I replied I wanted to flip, end over end during the sixty seconds. We pushed ourselves from the aircraft as one unit and began to roll.

The sixty-seconds passed quickly as we raced toward the ground. I experienced a painful sensation in my groin when the parachute opened. We decelerated quite abruptly and the strap under my crotch pulled taut, crushing everything in its path. I looked toward the sea once I was over the initial shock to my body. The beauty of Mother Nature's brilliant splendor surrounded me.

The instructor asked me if I wanted to maneuver the parachute. I declined and asked him to make the ride interesting. He did just that by turning us swiftly in one direction and then in the other direction. The sensation in my stomach was thrilling. I felt weightless while turning around the vortex of the parachute.

I soon asked my partner to simply descend slowly. The view was spectacular. I inhaled the clean ocean air deeply into my lungs. I looked toward the sky after we landed safely and watched as another airplane approached the drop-zone. I immediately wanted to get back into the airplane and jump again.

I inquired as to how one became a professional skydiver only moments after my natural high subsided. I felt the need to jump from an airplane on my own. The instructor told me I had to train by taking many jumps and several classes. I learnt it cost thousands of dollars to become certified. I did not have the money at the time, so I headed back to Brad's home in Tampa with dissatisfaction for the tandem experience.

I told Brad and his family about my experience skydiving that afternoon. Brad was excited for me, but thought my behavior was reckless. I talked to my parents on the phone and spoke to them about my day. My father said he could not understand why anyone would want to jump from a perfectly good airplane, because of his career as a fighter pilot.

My father's humor simply masked the concern my parents had for me. They knew I had stopped taking my medications while in New York. I departed from Tampa the next day and returned to Santa Fe. I was very hopeful for a new beginning as I drove the three days to New Mexico. I was unaware a simple television commercial would change my life and location once again.

The Whole Truth and Nothing but?

I sat idly after my return to Santa Fe and attempted to plan my next avenue to a successful acting career. I soon viewed an advertisement for the United States Army on the television while sitting on my parents couch. I watched intently as soldiers jumped from a military C-130 airplane. It looked very much like sky diving to me. The commercial showed many tough and determined soldiers carrying rifles and gear. The advertisement explained successful basic training graduates would receive a thirteen thousand dollar bonus. The commercial stirred me. I wanted the adventure and money the United States Army was offering.

I was at the Army recruiter's office the next morning. I told the recruiter of my true desire to serve in the United States Army. He was excited to hear my enthusiasm. We talked about the Army and what it had to offer me. The recruiter then proceeded to ask me a series of personal questions. He even inquired as to whether I had ever been prescribed antidepressants. I told him I had, but was not taking any at the time. The recruiter paused for a moment. He peered at me intensely and proceeded to explain I could not join the United States Army with any prior depressive history in my life. Thus, after another moment's pause, he asked me again "have you ever taken antidepressants?" I hesitated, but answered "no."

I pondered as to why my previous depression would be important to the United States Army. Nonetheless, I drove to the Army's military testing center in Albuquerque the next day. The recruiter called soon after my test with the result and told me I had scored 98%. I was in Albuquerque within a week, where I took my oath to serve in the United States Army and was sworn-in. The recruiter proceeded to take my picture in front of the American flag. I was very proud to be joining the dedicated men and women of the United States military. The military personnel I had known as a young man were outstanding human beings. My father was my hero and I hoped to make him proud of me.

My father was supportive of my decision. We were both excited for my new career in the Army. He and I ran five miles a day before my departure to basic training. We performed push-ups and sit-ups during the lengthy run. I knew the Army desired my physical abilities, so I trained to be all that I could be. I was physically fit and ready.

I flew from Albuquerque, New Mexico to Atlanta, Georgia not long after taking my oath to serve in the United States Army. I boarded a bus in Atlanta and was driven to Fort Benning, Georgia soon after my arrival. There were several other new Army recruits on the same bus. We talked about the adventures that awaited us at basic training. I told them about my sky diving experience and they were all ready to jump from an airplane with me. We were very excited to be in the United States Army.

The new recruits were given an introduction to the United States Army within the walls of a small brick building at Fort Benning. It was late in the evening as we fifty recruits awaited our destiny. We sat quietly with three drill sergeants present. They were enjoying a Dallas Cowboy's football game on a television. The new recruits were ordered into a meeting hall after two hours. We were escorted to the hall and ordered to take a seat. A colonel soon entered the room and greeted us. He talked about what the Army expected from its new recruits. The colonel then left the room. Before exiting, he told us not to fall asleep.

It was twelve thirty a.m. We had all flown from our home cities early that morning. The colonel was absent for an hour. Many of the new recruits closed their eyes and subsequently fell into a deep sleep. I caused pain in my hands, in order to stay awake, by pinching the soft flesh between my index finger and thumb. This kept me alert while waiting for the colonel to return.

The colonel discovered many of the recruits had fallen asleep when he re-entered the room. He then proceeded to shout for everyone to get on his hands and knees. We performed diamond push-ups for thirty minutes. I was extremely angry with the new recruits who had given-in to sleep. I considered them weak. I believed I would play the role of an exceptional soldier.

We were then ordered to stand in a line where we were to be issued our military uniforms. The drill sergeants went through our personal belongings as we waited. They discarded all sharp objects and even aspirin. The drill sergeants relieved every new recruit of these items. They then issued us our gear and we placed it neatly into a large duffel bag. We were then taken to our barracks.

The new recruits were ordered to find a cot and stow our gear. We then performed push-ups and scissor kicks for an hour. We were taken to the dining hall after our early morning physically demanding regimen. It was four a.m. after we finished eating. The recruits were taken back to the barracks and told that "PT" (Physical Training) was imminent. I decided to lay on my cot until the drill sergeants returned. There was no pillow, so I rolled my jeans and placed them under my head.

I was startled from sleep by loud shouting within an hour. The drill sergeants screamed, while banging trashcan lids against the walls of the barracks. They ordered the new recruits to stand to attention in front of our cots. We were ordered to get into our physical training uniform and then taken to a large running track. The new recruits performed physical training for an hour. We ran the track four times, completing one mile. The drill sergeants ordered us to do push-ups, scissor kicks, and sit-ups for the remainder of physical training. They then ordered the new recruits to proceed to chow hall for our morning meal. I had eaten just hours before, but found I was already famished.

The new recruits were ordered back to our barracks once we had finished eating. We shaved and showered at a normal pace. I unfolded and dressed into my camouflage battle dress uniform. I was then ordered to polish my combat boots. The drill sergeants instructed the new recruits on how to properly polish our boots. I worked on mine until I could see my own reflection in the polished black leather. We were told to keep our combat boots neatly polished at all times. The first week of basic training was spent doing such activities. We performed physical training, ate, polished our combat boots, and ate again.

All of the new recruits were measured for our class-A mess-dress uniform during the first week. The drill sergeants ordered the new recruits to exit the building after our measurements were recorded. I passed a soldier from down-range who was wearily sitting on the floor. He looked at me and quietly said, "quit now while you still can." I thought he was joking. I wanted to be a great soldier in the United States Army and quitting never crossed my mind. Our company of new recruits was taken down-range two days later.

The new recruits were ordered into cattle-cars on the morning of our eighth day. We all piled into the old, smelly cattle-cars (which had at one time been used to haul steer) and proceeded down-range to train. We arrived at our new barracks fifteen minutes later. A drill sergeant immediately started shouting in my face as I exited the cattle-car. I did not know what was occurring before two drill sergeants were yelling at me. I grabbed my duffel bag and ran toward where the drill sergeants were pointing.

The new recruits were ordered to perform push-ups, scissor kicks, and sit-ups. We did scissor-kicks for thirty minutes. This exercise was followed by more push-ups and sit-ups. The drill sergeants then yelled for half of the recruits to grab their own duffel bag and the duffel bag of the man next to him. We were ordered to lift both duffel bags above our head. The weight of each duffel bag was approximately fifty pounds. The drill sergeants became enraged when we failed to lift both duffels above our head. They ordered me to do this repeatedly until I could not even hold onto the bag itself.

I did my best to excel by doing exactly what I was told. Many new recruits were vomiting all around me. I did not regurgitate my own breakfast somehow. The drill sergeants screamed at us while we performed these exercises until dusk. One drill sergeant lost his voice, thus he sucked on lemons in order to regain his ability to yell. I was exhausted when a drill sergeant approached me and yelled, "The Army will break you down and build you back-up again!"

The drill sergeants finally ordered the new recruits into the barracks, where we stripped from our camouflage battle dress uniform. They screamed for us to take a fifteen-second shower. We then had fifteen-seconds to shave. We were ordered into the living area of the barracks and told to pick-up our duffel bag. I lifted the duffel over my head while still in the nude. The recruits were then ordered to run laps around the barracks. We did so with our duffel bag above our head. The drill sergeants told us to drop the duffel and get on our stomachs. We proceeded to do push-ups, sit-ups, and scissor-kicks in the nude.

The drill sergeants yelled at the new recruits to find a cot and stow our gear after two hours of performing these exercises. My mania helped me to endure the exercises, but I became suicidal during the hour of downtime. My manic and depressive episodes of the past five years reoccurred during the first day down-range at basic training. Suicide had never been an alternative to life for me until basic training with the United States Army.

It became all too clear to me why the Army recruiter asked me about my prior history with depression. The drill sergeant's harsh sentiment of "break you down" kept running through my mind. I was twenty-seven years old. The fact I cut upon my own flesh and past difficulties in my previous career had already broken me down. The United States Army's desire to "build you back-up again" was no longer a possibility for me without the assistance of psychotropic medications.

Our company was allowed to sleep for five hours the first night. I did not sleep, however. My mind was not racing any longer…it had stalled into oblivion. I decided suicide would give me the relief and release which I required. I proceeded to the bathroom in the early morning hours, where I was determined to shatter the mirror and slit my throat. Further depression set-in when I discovered the mirror was actually polished metal. I went back to my cot and lay down again. I tried to think of another way to end my life as I stared into the cold, white ceiling for the remainder of the night.

Drill sergeants entered our barracks at five a.m., shouting louder than the day before. We performed physical training exercises, ate, and marched in military formation throughout the day. We chanted "Kill, Kill, Kill with the Cold Blue-Steel" in cadence (The "Cold Blue -Steel" referred to the ominous hue of the M-16 rifle's fixed bayonet). I reflected on these words all day and night. It was not the enemy I was concerned with…I only wanted to destroy myself. The insanity of basic training only increased my true desire for death. Any mentally exhaustive stress at that point in my life would have caused suicidal ideations.

The rank I was issued when I enlisted in the Army was E-4 (Specialist), due to my college degree. The rank of a drill sergeant was usually E-5. The drill sergeants therefore hazed me harshly. They told the other new recruits my rank was "worthless." The drill sergeants told the E-1 (Privates) "they were more valuable to the U.S. Army than a Specialist." Their constant demeaning comments did not motivate me as they hoped for. Their attitude towards me completely exacerbated my already suicidal state of mind.

A drill sergeant noticed my rapid change in mood during our downtime on the second night. He tried to talk to me about the United States Army. He told me he was impressed with my physical training performance. The drill sergeant could not be too friendly; however, our short conversation did not appease me. My severe depression would not allow me to become the great soldier

I desired to be. My eyes never closed once we were ordered to "get some shut-eye" that evening.

I could not motivate myself to walk after dressing in to my physical training uniform the next morning. Self-harm was my only desire. I dropped to my knees before marching to the physical training track. I was sweating profusely, so I pulled the shirt from my body. All I could muster was to sit on the dingy, hardened pavement. A drill sergeant walked towards me and yelled "stand-up!" I looked at him with sincere regret and told him I was in need of a psychiatrist. Three drill sergeants were standing above me yelling within seconds of my uttering such a request. They did not want to hear about my mental problems…they wanted me to train.

The captain of the company soon emerged from his office after being told an E-4 Specialist was refusing to train. He approached me and I again explained my need to visit with a psychiatrist. I needed a doctor, but psychiatrists seemingly did not exist during basic training. The Army concentrated its efforts on training eighteen-year-old young men to become soldiers. The captain told me many new recruits go through a period of adjustment during basic training. I tried to explain my suicidal ideations. The captain did not blink an eye and ordered me to train. I could not move.

My state of mind did not deter the captain from placing me under house arrest, however. He explained my fate would be decided in a Court of the Armed Forces. I was to have a court-martial hearing. The drill sergeants made me live in a separate room (away from the company) before my trial. They often threatened to give me a "blanket party." I did not sleep for a week, fearing I would be beaten with socks containing several bars of soap.

There existed a private restroom attached to my quarters, which had an actual mirror. I contemplated shattering the polished glass and self-destructing. However, I decided against such an action, believing I would be discharged from the United States Army after my court-martial hearing. I attempted to grasp onto the hope I would be found not guilty and allowed to return home to my parents and much needed psychiatrist. I was even craving the necessary medications he would most definitely prescribe.

I tried to explain my present state of mind to the Judge Advocate General (JAG) during my trial. I told him about my history of cutting and depressive episodes. Further, I told the JAG my United States Army recruiter had knowingly suppressed the fact I had previously been prescribed antidepressants. The JAG convicted me of two military disciplinary articles an hour later. I pleaded "no-contest" and was given my punishment. The Army stripped me of my E-4 rank, all pay, and sentenced me to twenty-eight days in the brig (military prison).

Two drill sergeants immediately placed my hands behind my back and used a pair of handcuffs to bind my wrists. They then shackled my feet with a two-foot length of chain and a cuff around each ankle. The captain walked beside me as I was escorted to a government vehicle. He assured me I would be discharged from the United States Army after completing my incarceration in the brig. The captain's words did not ease my level of anxiety, however.

I was driven to the Naval Base in Pensacola, Florida, since Fort Benning had no brig. It was a long drive from Georgia to

Pensacola. I was still shackled as I sat in the back seat of the vehicle for hours. The drill sergeants were amused with my situation. We arrived at the Naval Base in Pensacola four hours later. It was nine p.m. The drill sergeants had one last chuckle as they departed. I was processed into the brig after their vehicle exited the locked garage.

VI. Incarceration

The Brig and Bible

I was allowed one phone call after being processed into the brig. I called my parents and apologized to my father. I was certain I had disappointed him. It was an emotional phone call. I tried to explain the circumstances of my situation during our short conversation. My parents were extremely concerned and confused.

I was taken to my holding cell after the five-minute phone call ended. The cell was six feet wide and ten feet in length. The only door was made entirely of shatterproof glass. The brig was dimly lit with the glow of red lights during the night. No other light was visible. I stared at the red lights for hours while sitting on the cold concrete floor of my small cell.

Bright florescent lights illuminated my cell at five thirty a.m. the following morning. I moved from the floor to my bed as a guard approached the cell. He told me to stand in front of the door, where I was to clearly state my name and social security number. I did so and he told me this was the regulation at five thirty a.m. each morning. The guard then left. I sat for a further thirty minutes until he delivered a breakfast tray to my cell.

My tray was cleared thirty minutes later. I sat idly on my cot for five hours. At eleven a.m., the same guard delivered a lunch tray. I ate and again my tray was cleared. I sat for another five hours. At five p.m. I was given my last tray of food for the day. I sat until the bright florescent lights were replaced by the soft, red glow that dimly illuminated the brig. I spent the entire day judging myself harshly for my failure in the United States Army, and did not sleep that night.

Florescent lights replaced the dim red glow at five thirty a.m. the following morning. I was standing in front of the shatterproof glass door already. I announced my name and social security number when the guard approached my cell door. My breakfast was delivered at six a.m. It was only my second day, but I knew the routine for any given day of solitary confinement in the brig. An hour passed when the guard returned to my door. He told me I was moving cells.

I was relieved to be leaving the six feet by ten feet cell. He opened my door and we walked five feet. He told me to enter the neighboring six feet by ten feet cell. However, this cell did not have a shatterproof glass door. The new door was solid steel and had a small, steel-mesh glass window. There existed a single opening (the size of a food tray) which locked from the outside. I did not know how long the cell was to be my home.

An inmate from general population was mopping the floor outside my cell that morning. He greeted me as I peered through the small window of my door. I was barely able to audibly hear the inmate as he spoke to me through the hardened glass window. He told me he would give the guards a *Bible* for me to read. The inmate expressed the sentiment I would "need it" as he departed. A guard delivered a small *Bible* to my cell an hour after the inmate's promise. I spent hours peering through the small, hardened glass window of my cell door. I eventually sat down on my cot and opened the small *Bible*.

I had nothing to do, and all day to do it. I decided to discover what the *Bible* had to offer, so I sat at my small desk and began to read the *Old Testament*. I read the *Bible* all day, starting with *Genesis*. I asked the guard if I could have a pen or pencil when he delivered my evening tray of food. He returned with a red pen later that evening. My *Bible* was large enough to underline certain passages and to write notes to myself. I desired to find hope within the many pages of my small *Bible*. I truly did need it.

My cell had a small desk with a retractable circular disk for a seat. The toilet had no seat and was firmly bolted to the concrete floor next to the desk. My cot was against the back wall. Above the bed was another small, steel-mesh glass window. It was four inches wide and three feet in length. I could see the world beyond my cell, while peering through the thin window. I often stared at the green trees and tall grass, moving occasionally in the breeze of the Florida coast. I resented the concrete brick walls that confined me from the earth's splendor and beauty. I simply desired to feel the warm wind again... gently caressing the small hairs of my neck.

I never laid in bed, or slept during the day. A guard would often walk past the small opening in the door and ask me for my name and social security number. I was told during my intake processing an inmate was reprimanded if he was caught sleeping during the day. I did not want to upset any of the guards. I was also told my sentence would be reduced by two days for "good behavior." I obeyed all protocol while in solitary confinement, due to this incentive.

During my third day, I asked the same inmate mopping outside my cell how long I could expect to be in the six feet by ten feet cell. I was able to understand he had spent eight days in the cell. I was concerned for how the small space, concrete walls, and living conditions would affect my mental state. Solitary confinement was crushing to my soul. Depression was reaping its usual effect on me.

I desired to run free and smell the freshly cut grass of my youth. Thinking I could be in the cell for another five days was inconceivable. I tried not to think about the additional twenty days in general population. My only possession was a small copy of the *Bible*, which I read with verbosity.

A Gift from God

I received a gift from God on my fourth day in solitary confinement. The brig alarm sounded in the afternoon and a guard approached my cell. He told me the building was to be evacuated. The guard unlocked my door and escorted me, along with the other inmates, to the outside perimeter. It was secured by a ten feet high fence, topped with razor wire.

I inhaled my first breath of fresh air in four days and embraced the serenity of the outside world. *God*, in his infinite generosity, then opened the heavens and it began to rain heavily. I allowed the moist droplets of rain to fall upon my face while gazing into the gray sky above. I thanked God for his gifts. I was beginning to feel truly blessed to be alive when the alarm ceased to ring and I was taken back to solitary confinement.

I was distracted from further reading the *Bible* on my fifth day in the small cell. A new neighbor moved into the six feet by ten feet cell next to mine. He screamed throughout the day. I could hear him pacing the floor for hours on end. The inmate who mopped the floor outside of my cell explained the person had been taken from general population for starting a fight with another inmate. The guards moved him to a solitary confinement cell as punishment. Listening to him scream was a punishment for me as well.

I finished reading the *Bible's Old Testament* before leaving solitary confinement. I was taken to general population after seven days. Walking was not a luxury while in the six feet by ten feet cell. It felt good to stretch my legs while walking the thirty paces to the general population quarters. The gray room consisted of twelve neatly dressed cots, two bathroom stalls, and two showers. I discovered how we inmates occupied our time later that afternoon.

The other inmates taught me the cleaning routine. We scrubbed the toilets, showers, and mopped the floor of the brig all afternoon. Cleaning a dirty toilet was humbling. I laughed to myself as I realized there were at least no toilet seats to scrub. The brig shined like a well-polished combat boot after four hours of scrubbing, cleaning, and mopping. The other inmates and I finished our duties at four thirty p.m. and were taken to dinner at five p.m. We always marched in a single file line, going to, and coming back from the chow hall.

The other inmates and I read, or talked about the *Bible* after dinner. I found most of them had built a relationship with God while in the brig. Those of us who were even slightly religious had a prayer meeting before bed. I enjoyed the silent moments of reflection. I was beginning to gain faith and hope in something more than just myself. I did not sleep during my first night in general population. I spent the hours staring into the soft, red glow of my own personal abyss.

The brig's fluorescent lights illuminated at five thirty a.m. the following morning. I took a shower and shaved until six a.m. Athlete's foot was a problem in the brig, so I wore military issued flip-flops when not in uniform. My United States Army camouflage battle dress uniform was worn during all of the daily duties and throughout my solitary confinement. I went to chow hall with the other inmates at six a.m. The food was descent and there was plenty of it. We returned to the general population quarters at six thirty a.m. I organized my footlocker between seven and eight a.m. My uniform, socks, underwear, and shirts were all expected to be neatly folded and properly stowed.

The other inmates and I mopped the floors, cleaned the showers, and scrubbed the toilet stalls at eight a.m. I scrubbed toilets while the other inmates cleaned elsewhere. My challenging duties were gladly interrupted when we were escorted to lunch at noon. I returned to my new home after lunch, where I found the other inmates collecting the cleaning supplies. I asked what our next scheduled duties were. They replied we were to clean the whole area again. Thus, I scrubbed toilets for the entire afternoon. I learned how to properly scrub a toilet and mop a floor while in the brig.

I had two hours of downtime every evening in general population, which did not include any outdoor visits. I began to read the *New Testament*, which I read slowly. I found the *New Testament* to be more inspiring than the *Old Testament*. I read the words of Jesus Christ and was amazed. I found Jesus Christ's concepts of "Love" and "Forgiveness" to be inspirational while reading. My continued discovery into the *Bible* truly helped me to survive my twenty-six days of confinement. I finished both the

Old Testament and *New Testament* before being released from the brig after twenty-six days.

I completely understood I had broken my contract with the United States Army. I was convicted, sentenced, punished, and served my time. My only thoughts were on the captain's assurance I would be going home after my confinement. The same two drill sergeants were parked in the locked inner garage on the day of my release from the brig. They did not handcuff me for the drive back to Fort Benning, Georgia, however.

I stared through the dirty window of the government vehicle's back seat while being escorted back to Fort Benning. I felt like a child who wakes with great anticipation early on Christmas morning. The outside world seemed more beautiful than I had remembered. All of the earth's colors were brilliant. The smell of the clean ocean air was intoxicating. Even the long stretch of highway and its dingy black pavement between freedom and me was a comfort. My depression lifted and I was pleased to be alive again.

The drill sergeants and I stopped at a fast food restaurant for lunch halfway between the brig and Fort Benning. I ordered and realized my wallet was still in the government vehicle. The drill sergeants gave me the keys to the car, so I could acquire money from my duffel bag. I thought of stealing it while opening the trunk of the car and driving away. I simply procured my wallet instead. I went back into the restaurant and paid for my food. My greasy cheeseburger tasted like filet-mignon, which was washed-down with bubbling carbonated cola! The crispy French fries melted in my mouth. Once we were finished with our fine dining the drill sergeants and I continued our travels to Georgia.

We arrived at Fort Benning later that evening. The drill sergeants escorted me to the barracks. They left me outside the captain's office and proceeded inside. A young soldier, who was running past, asked me to hold his M-16 rifle. He said he would be back in a minute. A drill sergeant walked towards me a moment later and calmly said "put the rifle down on the ground." I pondered as to whether he knew something I did not, and placed the M-16 rifle onto the dirty pavement.

The captain emerged from his office with a serious look upon his face as the drill sergeant took the weapon. He approached me with two drill sergeants following him. The captain looked me straight in the eye and explained the United States Army had decided to "restart" me. I was confused and asked him to repeat what he had said. He told me a new company was starting basic training the next day and I would be joining them.

My heart raced during the short second it took for me to understand the captain's words. I immediately and uncontrollably started to beat myself in the face. My fists pounded my facial flesh with force, repeatedly. I ran toward the nearest wall and slammed my head into its immovable, hardened brick. My mind destroyed any rational thought. I was happy to be alive earlier in the day and now desired to destroy myself. I was experiencing a complete mental upheaval. The entire company of soldiers watched as I beat myself. Four drill sergeants finally restrained my arms from further damaging my face.

The drill sergeants carried me by all four limbs to a nearby room. It was the room I had previously been confined within (the room with a glass mirror in its bathroom). The drill sergeants placed me onto the floor and, thinking I was calm, left the room. A new recruit immediately entered the room. The recruit found me continuing to beat my face with furious fists until I could not muster the strength to throw my closed hand into my head with such ferocity any longer.

Depression of no type that I had ever experienced encompassed me. My survival instinct for mania was upon me. I wanted to shatter the mirror and cut my flesh apart. I desired a release of endorphins. The captain entered after a short time, in order to see what I was doing. He talked to me in a soft voice and told me to sleep. I lacked the ability to move, so I did as he asked.

I awoke the next morning to find a different recruit watching over me. He promptly exited the room and a drill sergeant entered. The captain then escorted a one-star general into my room. The general looked at my face and directly said, "I don't want this man in my Army." The general walked away shaking his head with disgust. I did not personally know the general, but he reminded me of my father. I reflected upon the general's apparent disappointment with me. I understood I failed the United States Army and my country.

A drill sergeant escorted me to the base psychiatrist an hour later. The psychiatrist called my previous psychiatrist in Santa Fe and asked him for my past diagnosis. He soon after handed me a prescription for an antidepressant. The drill sergeant and I filled the prescription. He watched me take the antidepressant before returning to the barracks. I was hopeful the medications would instantly resolve my severe depression and suicidal ideations.

The drill sergeant asked me why I had not simply gone "AWOL." I told him I was not a coward… I was mentally ill. Running from my commitment to the United States Army was not an option for me. I told him, I truly respected the young men and women whom he had been training to become soldiers. The drill sergeant said that, physically, I had great potential. He did not understand the mental illness of which I suffered.

All that remained for me to do was to take a discharge physical, and finish the necessary discharge paperwork. I sat in the back of a military truck with five other new recruits who were also being discharged. None of them had been court-martialed or confined in the brig. I did not concern myself with the reasons for their discharge, however. I focused on returning home alive. I received an Entry Level Separation from the United States Army. The Army designated an Entry Level Separation discharge to new recruits who had been in the military for less than ninety days.

I was on an airplane to Albuquerque, New Mexico a day later. My parents met me at the gateway. My mother and father became very concerned for my mental health as they looked upon my damaged face. I told my parents everything that had occurred at basic training, and the brig, during our drive to Santa Fe. My father explained he was not disappointed in me... I was, however. My mother was simply relieved I was home safely. They were both supportive. I thanked them for their generosity, and slept for two days once in the comfort of my parent's home.

VII. Cycling

Motorcycles

I returned from basic training in October of 1997. My failure in the United States Army affected me terribly. I had always believed I could control my mental illness solely with my own efforts. My military experience taught me differently. My mood swings during basic training were life threatening and I needed professional assistance with controlling them. I knew medications were necessary for my mental health to become more stable.

My mother was a psychotherapist at a mental health facility in Santa Fe at the time. She dealt with patients whom had a similar diagnosis as mine. My mother told me about a psychiatrist who visited the facility and often prescribed medications for its clients. She described my symptoms to the psychiatrist not long after my return from Fort Benning. My mother then asked me to visit his office with the hope I would be receptive.

I met with the psychiatrist a week later and talked with him about my past difficulties. However, I failed to tell the psychiatrist about my extreme highs. I was not even aware of the clinical term for mania, or manic episode. My new psychiatrist concluded I suffered from severe depression with the information that I did divulge. He prescribed a higher dosage of antidepressant than I had previously been taking. My mood became more stable after a month on the antidepressant. I spent time with my parents in Santa Fe, and at our family cabin. The mountains were a good place for me to recuperate and the cabin always cleared my mind of the past.

I occupied my time in between psychiatric appointments as a carpenter for my parents in Santa Fe. Their home became a living testament to the beauty of my willow stick stylish creations. I began with the master bedroom where I re-built my previous shutters. I then constructed shutters for the other two windows in their bedroom. A lumber store near town sold willow sticks and I purchased fifteen bundles that year.

My mother contracted me to build a large shutter for the sliding glass door in the guest bedroom. I decided to suggest building items for more areas of the house, which might be enhanced by my furniture style. I re-constructed five of their interior doors. I built a six feet tall folding screen for the back door. I decided the guest bathroom and kitchen were in need of new cabinets, so added the willow stick additions there. I then built a stylish dining room table for my father's birthday.

I noticed the wall next to the dining room table was bare and lifeless, thus I constructed a large mirror to hang in the dining room area. The bar seemed empty and cold as well, so I built a mirror to place above it. I even constructed doors for the television and stereo cabinets. I soon convinced myself others would desire my style of furniture.

An acquaintance of mine, who was familiar with my carpentry work, told me about a client of his. He described her as a "trust fund baby" with expensive taste. I was introduced to the woman and she commissioned me for two large folding screens. I returned to my parent's garage and built two six feet wide by eight feet tall screens in three days. I delivered them four days after my initial conversation with woman and she handed me a check. The price we had agreed upon was $3,500. I placed the screens where the woman requested and departed with an enormous smile upon my face.

I was taking my antidepressant as prescribed, but always became hypomanic during the process of carpentry. I became invigorated by my heightened state of mind and ability to accomplish a great deal of work. I sold my pick-up truck after completing the woman's screens and used my profits to purchase a Jeep Wrangler. The summer of 1998 was rapidly approaching when I departed for our family cabin, in order to build a new deck.

I demolished the old deck after realizing it was rotting from underneath. I drove my Jeep from Santa Fe to the cabin with five loads of lumber within a week. The smell of the freshly cut pine and clean mountain air was intoxicating while driving my new vehicle without its hardtop. I was always eager to unload the materials and begin building.

However, a new state of mania ensued while building the deck at the cabin. I would build the deck in my mind while I lay in bed at night. I planned exactly where to start the next morning while simply waiting for the bright sun to rise. I rapidly constructed a ten feet by twenty-five feet deck from first light until it was pitch black outside.

I stood upon my beautiful and functional new deck with pride after successfully finishing the project. It was a great accomplishment for me to construct on my own. I sat on the warm deck as the sun shined upon me and drank a cold beer. The cool hops tasted wonderful while relaxing. My flavorful reward always tasted better when enjoyed with sweat still upon my tanned brow and sawdust in my nostrils. I built a couch and two rocking chairs for the deck within a week. The summer passed quickly and I knew gainful employment would soon be necessary.

I rejoined my acquaintances at the restaurant where I had previously been a singing waiter. I had not been singing regularly since I had left New York. I soon discovered I was unable to sing very well while I attempted to project sound during a rehearsal. I immediately made an appointment to see my psychiatrist with the belief my medications were causing my difficulties vocalizing. He told me there was a possibility my current antidepressant may affect muscle tension in the vocal chords. I requested he prescribe me a different antidepressant during the session.

I was growing weary from the side effects, and completely discontinued my antidepressant soon after acquiring the new medication. I experienced a deep depression within a month. I began to rapid cycle and suffered a manic episode. I purchased my first of many motorcycles, a small 250 CC Honda Rebel.

I had never ridden a motorcycle and wanted to start on something I could physically handle. The 250 CC motorcycle cost me $4,000, which I charged on my credit card along with the necessary gear. I purchased a leather jacket, chaps, and gloves. I had simply purchased my own personal super hero costume. The salesperson tried to persuade me to buy a bigger bike, but I had made my decision to purchase the 250 CC Honda Rebel.

The salesperson quickly concluded I was a novice as I mounted the motorcycle. I could not figure out how to shift the bike into first gear, so he gave me the proper tutelage about the different gears. I probably weighed as much as the motorcycle with all of my leather gear on. I soon felt ridiculous while riding the highway from Albuquerque to Santa Fe. I was re-fueling later that day when a stranger shouted, "I hope that's your little brother's bike." I decided a bigger motorcycle was necessary before departing from the gasoline station.

I rode my Honda 250 CC Rebel to Albuquerque the next morning. The salesperson was happy to see me. He was pleased I wanted a bigger bike and delighted his commission would increase with my trade-in. I discovered a black Honda 750 CC while searching for the perfect motorcycle. I returned the 250 CC and rode-off on the 750 CC after charging another $4,000 to my credit card. Riding the Honda 750 CC was much more comfortable. However, I became obsessed with the desire for an even bigger motorcycle while gazing upon my newly acquired motorcycle the next day.

A week had not passed before I rode back into the Honda dealership. I described to the salesperson my need for a bigger motorcycle. He showed me a used Honda 1100 CC Shadow on the sales floor. My eyes glazed-over as I looked at the chrome details on the bike. There was only one flaw. The previous owner had painted his work logo on the gas tank. The salesperson told me I could buy the Honda 1100 CC for a reasonable price because of the personalized logo.

I had already spent $8,000 on obtaining the 750 CC, but did not hesitate and purchased the 1100 CC Shadow. I solved the logo problem by sanding the paint from the gas tank. The bare steel underneath was beautiful. I proceeded to remove each baffle (muffler) from its pipe. The 1100 CC Shadow was absurdly loud after I completed this simple manipulation. I reveled in the sound and how it annoyed others. My mania was the same volume as the motorcycle.

Crash

My bipolar disorder had always been damaging to my health, but I suffered from it monetarily as well. I was ruminating daily, regarding my failings with the United States Army and began to do so after spending $13,000 in one week on motorcycles. My mood was changing rapidly. The manic wave I was riding crashed heavily into the shore and I became deeply depressed. The fact I was not taking my prescribed medications only exacerbated my already distorted state of mind.

I began to self-destruct and cut upon my body again. I used scissors to cut my upper arms while standing before my bathroom mirror, hoping to create scars. I pressed forcefully against the blade and deep into my skin. Blood flowed heavily down my arms as I pulled the scissors across my flesh. The cutting was not random. I created tattoos on each arm after cutting two long wounds across each bicep. Once again, my delusional mind immediately experienced relief from any depression.

I wiped the blood away with bathroom tissue while cutting. The toilet became my receptacle for any evidence of blood. I did not want my parents to see what I had done and believed they would not notice if my upper arms were covered with a shirt during the process of healing. However, my father heard the constant flushing of the toilet and walked downstairs to see if I was all right. He looked at my arms and became very concerned. He was not emotional, but simply methodical, as we cleansed and bandaged my wounds.

My father insisted I go to bed, but I remained sleepless for the remainder of the night. My father did not sleep either. We talked at length about my self-destructive behaviors the next morning. I confessed I had discontinued my medications, so my parents insisted on watching me swallow my prescribed dosage that evening. I took the medications and continued to do so for the remainder of the summer. I still owned my Jeep, but preferred riding the motorcycle. I rode my bike every opportunity I had. I was beginning to enjoy my life again. However, I was uncertain if contentment was the state of mind I was ready to embrace.

I was feeling healthier, due to my medication, and decided to continue pursuing my acting career. Royal Caribbean Cruise Lines often held auditions throughout the United States. Their main office was in Miami, so I decided to take a more direct route and drive to Florida. I called the production company and they arranged an audition date for me during the next workweek. Thus, I loaded my Jeep and drove east the next day. I planned to visit my brothers and an old friend during my trip to Miami.

I started driving from Santa Fe to Michigan at five a.m. I drove non-stop and arrived at my friend's home twenty-eight hours later. I discovered I had forgotten to bring along my antidepressant medication while unpacking my suitcase. I was returning to Santa Fe after my upcoming audition, so did not worry a great deal about my mental health. I drove to Scott's home in Virginia after my short visit to Michigan.

Scott's family and I enjoyed each other's company for two days, and then I headed for Miami. It was November in Florida and very sunny. I had already been informed as to the location of the audition and arrived early. I sang *Transformation* from *Jekyll and Hyde*. It was an awkward moment between the director and me. I started as Jekyll and as the song progressed truly transformed into Hyde. I was manic and became a raving lunatic in the truest sense. My performance was very convincing, but not appropriate.

I came to my senses as the director was dismissing me and asked if she wanted to hear something else. The director said my voice did not meet the vocal range of the contract she had available. I asked her to play the highest note necessary. She did and I sang it clearly. We went through a few songs and I sang them well. The director was surprised and asked me why I had auditioned with *Jekyll and Hyde*. I replied I believed *Transformation* displayed my range of acting abilities. She agreed, but admitted my performance was too frightening for an initial audition. The director offered me the contract nonetheless and told me rehearsals began in December. I was elated. The contract was for two shows on the cruise liner *Rhapsody of the Seas*. I was to be performing on the high seas again.

I drove from Miami to Tampa, where I stayed with Brad and his family for two days. We went to Busch Gardens both days and I rode the roller coasters with my young adventurous nephew. I wanted to see my parents before December arrived, so I left Florida and drove to New Orleans. I drank the local beer on Bourbon Street for an hour and then returned to my hotel room. I woke at nine a.m. the following day and arrived in Santa Fe twenty-four hours later. Mania and carbonated soda kept me awake during the long drive across the southern United States.

I did not restart my medication regimen when I arrived back in Santa Fe because of my heightened state of mind. Manic was the mood that my distorted mind desired. The high I always experienced was non-negotiable. There was no return as far as I was concerned. I was riding a wave, which I believed would never crash into the wet sandy beach. Becoming a super hero seemed possible during a full-blown manic episode. The thought of depression never entered my mind, even though I had crashed many times in the past. My mental health was not a concern of mine as I prepared for my next acting contract.

Rehearsals for the *Rhapsody of the Seas* were held in Miami. I was in a heightened state of mind, but made a good impression on the other cast members. My demeanor was very professional during rehearsals. I worked hard on my songs and dance choreography. The director appreciated my energy and hard work to learn the two shows. Our cast completed the short rehearsal process and we flew to California.

San Pedro, California was the port for the *Rhapsody of the Seas*. My experience with Royal Caribbean Cruise Lines was much different from that with Norwegian Cruise Lines. I had a single room on the *S.S. Norway* and lived quite comfortably. The *Rhapsody* assigned me a roommate. Sharing a small cabin with another person proved inconvenient. My roommate was from Manchester City, England. I was twenty-nine and did not cope well while cohabitating with him.

My roommate was quite the lady's man. He was a dancer and physically fit. Women liked his charm and English accent. He and another dancer started to date soon after our contracts began. They proceeded to use our room to have sex in every day. I was forced to entertain myself quite often while they were in the room. Thus, I went to the crew bar every day. The *Rhapsody of the Seas* bar did not have the jovial spirit of the *S.S. Norway* crew bar. In fact, there was rarely another person present besides the bartender and myself.

I was designated to gather a portion of the new passengers at their required emergency boat drill station of the ship during the first day of every cruise to the Mexican Caribbean. I met a nice passenger girl and her family during a boat drill two months into my contract. They thought I was funny and invited me to have dinner with them. I declined after explaining the crewmembers were not permitted to eat in the passenger dining rooms.

I met the young woman while walking the ship a few days later and she once again invited me to dinner. The girl explained she failed to understand why a cast member could not simply entertain a few willing passengers. I found her logic to be very similar with my own. Further, the girl was attractive and I desired to become close with her. I accepted the young woman's invitation and joined her in the dining room that evening.

I received a great deal of attention from the young woman and her family. My mood subsequently flourished into my previous altered state of hypomania. My behavior became grandiose. I was jovial, funny, and loud. The family told me how pleased they were I had joined them. The beautiful girl found me charming and I returned her sentiment by becoming even more boisterous.

My behavior drew a great deal of attention from the other passengers and my fellow crewmembers. The servers in the dining room recognized me from the shows. They knew I was part of the theater cast and not permitted to eat in the passenger dining rooms. I was aware of this fact, but did not care. "So fire me" was my attitude. I was high on life and planned to join my new friends for dinner the next evening.

I was even more grandiose the following night while eating dinner with my new friends. My mood digressed from hypomania into full-blown mania within twenty-four hours. I was confronted by a dining room crewmember on this particular occasion. He was finished tolerating my escapade. I exclaimed loudly, if he was so inclined, the captain could join me while eating and drinking with new friends in the dining room. My larger than life behavior only continued after dinner.

I proceeded to steal a cigar from the captain's personal cigar bar. I smoked the cigar throughout the ship with the beautiful girl. I knew all too well it was to be my last night and decided to end my days on the *Rhapsody of the Seas* with flare. The young woman and I parted company after midnight. I continued to drink until sunrise, however. I began to pack all of my possessions at dawn.

A fellow crewmember knocked on my door at eight a.m. He told me the ship's captain wanted to see me. I was escorted to the captain's office and confronted by a panel of ship's officers upon entering. The captain sat in the middle of the table. He looked at me with anger in his eyes and asked me to explain my behavior. I responded I was simply "entertaining passengers." The captain told me my actions warranted a dismissal from the *Rhapsody of the Seas*. I agreed with him, was fired, and returned to my room in order to finish packing.

I found the beautiful young woman on an upper-deck of the ship before disembarkation. We embraced and I tearfully professed my love for her. She kissed me on the cheek and said farewell. I had only known her for a few days, but turned to gaze upon her one last time before leaving the *Rhapsody of the Seas*. I never saw the girl or her family again. My mania had once again drawn people to me, and pushed them away, all in the same breath.

VIII. True Love

Laura in Las Vegas

I flew from California to Santa Fe in March of 1999. My parents were concerned when I returned from my contract four months earlier than expected. I told them about my mishaps and they were understandably disappointed. However, I was not the least bit concerned about the manic behavior I had experienced while on the *Rhapsody of the Seas*. I simply went on with my life as if nothing had occurred. My mind's ability to suppress the truth and its quest for self-preservation was becoming even more adept and finely tuned.

I called an old acquaintance from the *S.S. Norway* a week after my return. I had not been in contact with Jan since 1995, and was hoping she might know of possible performance opportunities. She was living in Las Vegas, Nevada with her husband at the time. Jan asked me about my occupational conquests and I lied by telling her I was still thriving in show business. I inquired as to her status and asked Jan if there were any singing jobs in Las Vegas worth pursuing. She said there were.

Jan explained a Las Vegas talent agency, which she worked with, was hiring singers the following week. My mind raced with anticipation before we finished talking on the telephone. A week had not elapsed when I rode my motorcycle to Las Vegas. I auditioned for the talent agency two days after I arrived. I sang *Make them hear you* from the musical *Ragtime*. They heard me all right. My audition went well enough to secure employment as an opera singer in Las Vegas, Nevada.

My position with the talent agency was profitable. I was able to pay for rent and leisure comfortably. The rehearsal process began in April and I made friends with the other cast members. One woman stood alone as a possible candidate for dating. She was beautiful. I wanted to be Laura's friend and lover from the moment I laid eyes upon her. However, she had a boyfriend. We took our time getting to know one another as friends while rehearsals continued to progress.

Rehearsals were simple as we learned popular Italian Opera songs. I had sung a few of them while in college and my previous problems with diction were resolved. My desire to be intimate with Laura never ceased to exist. I watched intently whenever she sang. I hoped she would notice me while performing my songs. Laura's boyfriend came to visit her from Baltimore before rehearsals were completed. The other cast members liked him well enough, but I despised him. He was a good-looking Italian person in his early twenties. I thought of myself as inferior to him.

Laura's boyfriend returned to the east coast after a week and I tried to build upon my relationship with her. She and I started meeting after rehearsals, in order to have a drink and talk. She thought my motorcycle did not fit my personality. Laura was not yet fully aware my motorcycle was a reflection of my personality. Laura had no idea I was in love with her. I kept my feelings to myself, fearing she may possibly reject my sentiment.

The cast finished the rehearsal process and began performing at The Venetian Resort and Casino. It was a spectacular venue in which to sing. We performed Opera vignettes while strolling throughout the Grand Canal shops. Our cast dressed in seventeenth century costumes and sang songs for gathering crowds. Las Vegas was not Broadway, but I felt it was a step in the right direction.

The talent agency cast me as Casanova. My costume was beautiful and I played the part with enthusiasm. I wore knee-high white stockings with black loafers and a pair of blue pantaloons. My cream-colored shirt had an extravagantly ruffled collar typical of the era. My costume was completed with a blue knee length jacket and white-powdered wig. I perspired heavily while wearing the many layers. My skull was especially warm, so I decided to shave my head of all hair after the first day performing.

I had never fully shaven my head before and was shocked at how I appeared. My baldhead was as white as snow. It did not look very appealing to me, and I thought my chances of ever dating Laura where virtually impossible. The next day at work Laura surprised me when she commented I was a "handsome man." I was elated by her response. She complimented my appearance and I was grateful. The emotion I felt for Laura was that of complete infatuation.

Laura was just over five feet in height, with an athletic body. Her hair was sandy-blonde in color. I took great pleasure in looking at her beautiful face and its gentle features. Laura was the type of woman I had been waiting for all my life. Her compliment "handsome man" gave me the courage to further pursue her. Laura lived with several roommates, so we usually found ourselves at my apartment. We finally kissed after work one night and continued to do so for hours. Her lips were sweet and wonderfully soft. I desired to spend the remainder of my days on earth caressing her lips with mine.

Laura and I shared smiles across the crowds of people while at work. Laura was gorgeous and even more so while singing. I loved to watch her perform. She was very playful on-stage and off. Her personality was genuine and caring. I loved being in Laura's presence. She was my best friend and first true love. Laura moved into my apartment a month after we started dating. It was a remarkable moment for me. I had never lived with a girlfriend. None of my prior relationships seemed worthy of such a commitment.

Neither Laura nor I owned very many belongings, so our apartment consisted of a queen size mattress and portable stereo. We sat on the floor and listened to music during our first night of residing with one another. We drank wine and celebrated our life together. Laura and I were intimate for the first time that evening. She was a wonderful lover. I had never felt such rapture with a woman as I did with Laura. We were tender in each other's arms. My life seemed complete.

The next day I commented about our need for furniture and Laura agreed. I purchased furnishings on my first day free from work. I went shopping and acquired a new four-post bed. It was constructed of attractive gray metal. I also purchased a yard of white silk and draped it over the top of the four-posts. Laura loved it. I then purchased a white couch, love seat, television, and video cassette player. Laura and I spent most of our evenings together, simply enjoying our new possessions and each other. The apartment was comfortable and we called it home.

We lived in harmony for six months. This did not change the fact I had been steadily growing disillusioned with my singing job at the Venetian Hotel and Casino. My previous contracts were not lengthy. I was always happy to leave the ship, the tour, or summer stock after only a few months had elapsed. However, I did not want to end my relationship with Laura. My desire to change jobs and locations was secondary to my love for her.

Laura and I grew very close. She was everything I wanted in a friend and lover. My determination to continue our relationship was solidified when Laura's car lost all of its coolant and thus warped the engine's cylinders. A car dealership told Laura the repairs were to be very costly. My parents had given me their red Saturn automobile months earlier, so I lent it to Laura the day after her vehicle broke-down. She was thankful and drove it to work the next morning. I decided to permanently solve Laura's problem while she was working that day.

My mind began to race since I had discontinued my prescribed medications months before moving to Las Vegas, Nevada. I experienced a manic episode while shopping at a local automobile dealership. I purchased Laura a new blue convertible. I called her parents from the dealership and asked Laura's father for his blessings. I explained I planned to propose marriage to his daughter Laura. He was pleased I had called and gave me his consent. I drove the vehicle to the nearest jeweler once the dealership finished with the necessary paperwork.

I gazed upon many diamond rings while at the jewelry store. I also looked at rings with the inclusion of Laura's birthstone. I pondered upon which ring would best reflect my true love for Laura. I noticed a beautiful ring that revealed itself from under the glass counter. Small diamonds surrounded a radiant stone. I immediately purchased the ring and proceeded home.

I lowered the convertible roof of Laura's new car and then tied the ring to the rear-view mirror. The dealership had given me a large blue helium balloon, so I attached it to the passenger seat. Laura soon after passed me as she drove into our parking area. I exited the auto, ran toward her, and led Laura to her new car. She was in disbelief as I explained the car was hers. I asked Laura to sit in the driver's seat, whereupon she noticed the ring. She sat quietly as I proposed marriage to her. Laura was overwhelmed. She smiled and said "yes" to my proposal. Neither Laura nor I was concerned with my state of mind.

I plummeted into depression within a week of purchasing the automobile. I had tolerated my employment at The Venetian Resort and Casino in order to be with Laura every day, but became overwhelmed by my depression regarding work. This fact affected every other aspect of my life. Drinking alcohol became routine. I drank alcohol in moderation during the beginning of my relationship with Laura. However, after nine months in Las Vegas I pursued intoxication on a regular basis. I purchased a fresh twelve pack of beer every evening. Laura had two glasses of wine. She never confronted me about my drinking, however. My looming depression was never a topic of our lighthearted conversations either.

Laura and I often viewed movies during our evenings together. One such night we decided to view a dramatic film. I watched intently while drinking my usual amount of beer. The film affected both Laura and I. Laura explained she had faced similar trials in her past when the movie finished. Her story caused me to become very emotional and I immediately became withdrawn. I was not angry with Laura, but became extremely sad for her painful journey. Laura grew frightened by my silence as I sat quietly on the couch. I was unable to move as I stared at the empty far wall of our living room. Finally, I collapsed…mentally.

Destructive Love

I walked to the kitchen utensil drawer after a long moment of reflection. I found a sharp steak knife among the few forks and spoons. I proceeded to cut randomly at my arms and back while standing in the kitchen. Shock overcame Laura. She could not watch me destroy my flesh as I cut repeatedly.

Laura escaped to our bedroom. I ceased to tear my skin apart with the knife once she left the room. Mania was once again upon me. I spent a sleepless night while sitting on the white couch. I continued to stare at the empty walls for hours. I called my parents the following morning and told them what had occurred. They asked me not to hurt myself any further.

Laura woke the next morning and voiced her concern for me. She knew I had previous tendencies of self-destruction, but it became a horrid reality, which she was unable to understand. I never wished to hurt Laura. Mania and depression were aspects of my life, which I had never fully explained to her. I was in complete denial of the true consequences I faced without properly treating my mental illness.

I understood the necessity for mental health assistance as I looked into Laura's eyes that morning. Otherwise, I was certain I would never be granted the honor of gazing at her beautiful facial featured ever again. My parents arrived within twenty-four hours of our phone conversation. We all sat in the living area and talked about my future. My mother asked me to visit a psychiatrist. I agreed I needed professional help. We all thought it best for me to take a sabbatical from Las Vegas and seek the assistance of my previous psychiatrist in Santa Fe.

We packed my necessary belongings a day later. I called and made an appointment to see my psychiatrist for the following week. Laura decided she no longer wanted the blue convertible. She was making the payments after realizing I could not afford to purchase her the vehicle. Laura stayed at the apartment in Las Vegas and my parents escorted me to Santa Fe. I was hopeful of stability and became proactive in my desire to accept the necessary assistance for my mental illness.

My parents and I departed Las Vegas on a crisp March morning. My mother drove the car that my parents had driven to Las Vegas. My father was behind the wheel of the blue convertible, which my parents agreed to purchase, and I rode my motorcycle. We arrived in Santa Fe the next day. I honestly could not think of what had caused me to depart from Las Vegas, even though the cuts were still fresh upon my body. My mind was becoming increasingly more effective at de-rationalization, self-preservation, and displacing the negative aspects of my difficulties with sanity. Nevertheless, I met with my psychiatrist that week.

IX. Diagnosis

My Bipolar Illness

I reflected upon the turmoil of my life soon after departing from Las Vegas and Laura. Depression had not been an emotion that I suffered from during my youth. However, I often experienced deep depression in my twenties. Life seemed futile during periods of severe depression. Eating or brushing my teeth seemed pointless. I slept fourteen hours per day and rarely witnessed the sunrise or set. My family could not console me. I rarely broke into a smile. Drinking alcohol became an avenue that temporarily subdued my depressive moods. I was not aware it was a one-way street leading me into an even deeper crevasse. Moderation seemed to elude me and drinking heavily only exacerbated my depression. The alcohol would help with my self-abasement and ruminations for a short while. However, the result was always an intense level of mental anguish. Subsequently, my depression became life threatening.

I was prone to cutting upon my body as a necessity to relieve the depth of my depression. Mania was the desired result, which I pursued while bloodletting. I truly believed I was the most talented singer in the world while manic. I would sleep only three hours per night and accomplished a great deal of work while manic. Everyone was my friend, or so I thought.

Life was beautiful beyond words and anything seemed possible while manic. I believed death to be something the weak suffered from. I spent vast amounts of money on others and myself. I lived life as if there were no consequences to my actions. However, I always became deeply depressed after a manic episode had subsided. The reality of what I had done to myself and others resulted in an emotional tempest.

My manic driven ego was a double-edged sword during my acting career. I could not acquire employment without it and destroyed relationships because of it. I required a great amount of confidence when auditioning and performing. However, my constant struggles only became more intense, due to my inflated ego. I thrived on the level of grandiosity typical of the bipolar illness. I was larger than life when manic, but could not think of a reason to live within minutes of my euphoric delusions. These moods cycled rapidly and without warning. I lived two separate lives. Mania was my survival instinct and depression caused me to seek my own annihilation.

Depression never occurred while performing on stage. It was crucial for me to believe I was important to other people. However, I could not build upon any professional or friendly relationships because of my over-bearing hypomanic personality. I grew deeply depressed when I was not popular with the other cast members or women. Thus, I pushed people even further away with my constant mood cycles. I often judged myself harshly for my failings with work, friends, and girlfriends. An overpowering sense of worthlessness would always envelop me during periods of severe depression.

My mind functioned without the capacity to keep memories of my actions and their consequences. Life became irretrievably futile whenever I recalled the extreme behaviors of my past. Ruminations, concerning my failure in the United States Army, caused me to suffer an overwhelming amount of emotional pain. I often reflected on the intense mania and deep depression, which occurred simultaneously during basic training. I would experience a short respite from my negative self-image when hypomanic, or during a manic episode. This fact caused me to desire a constant manic state of mind.

I understood the symptoms of my illness, but never truly sought the assistance of professionals. During my first few years of drastic mood-swings, I was diagnosed with severe depression. However, I had not been completely honest with my psychiatrists. I did not want to face the reality of my illness, so I kept the difficult details to myself. I initially took the medications that I was prescribed. I always discontinued all prescriptions after my mental health improved. I truly ceased in my quest for mental health. I literally did not desire to swallow the truth, metaphorically or literally.

I conned myself into believing my mood changes were controllable. Depression was a part of my non-existent past when experiencing hypomania, or a full-blown manic episode. I did not fully understand the two poles of mania and depression was co-existing. I often acted abnormally by destroying myself, despite my desire for normalcy.

Type II

I visited my psychiatrist at his office after departing Las Vegas in March of 2000 with revitalized determination to seek assistance.

The psychiatrist diagnosed me as bipolar type II, due to my recent manic episode of cutting. He told me bipolar disorder was a mood disorder. He explained there was an imbalance of chemicals in my brain, which caused me to suffer from severe mood changes. I finally learned the medical term for my mental illness at the age of thirty.

My psychiatrist further explained the severity of my illness and its necessity for medications. He then prescribed a mood-stabilizer. My psychiatrist said it was an anti-seizure medication, which helped with manic episodes and severe mood swings. He also increased my previous dosage of antidepressant. I filled the prescriptions with great anticipation. However, weeks passed before I witnessed any relief from my self-destructive thoughts and behaviors.

I became frustrated with the process and side effects of my medications, as well. My parents often reminded me of the self-destructive tendencies which I previously exhibited and often followed through with. Their constant support reinforced my determination to seek assistance. I knew medications were to play an important role if I was to fight against, and survive my dangerous path to a brief existence.

I visited my psychiatrist every two weeks. He wanted to hear about my progress with the medications. We talked about side effects and dosage levels. My psychiatrist was very knowledgeable about my bipolar disorder. I was surprised by his candor. He was a sincere man. My psychiatrist gave me the impression he was truly concerned for my health. I was very fortunate to find such a compassionate psychiatrist.

I continued to talk with Laura on the telephone while residing in Santa Fe. My mental health was improving, but I missed her terribly. My mind soon forgave me for what I had done to my body. I tried not to focus on the rapid cycling that I had experienced in Las Vegas. This was in large part due to the effects of my medications. I decided to return to Las Vegas in July of the year 2000. I was convinced my future there would be new and improved. My thoughts were occupied with hopes for the many possibilities and a return to Laura.

My parents followed me back to Las Vegas, Nevada with my personal belongings in their vehicle. Laura had moved into a different apartment and we decided I could join her. I moved in with her when I returned. Laura and I rekindled our friendship and intimate relationship. She was relieved both my mind and body had healed. I was simply pleased she was in my life again. The fact Laura did not judge me for my past self-destructiveness was extremely important as well.

My previous singing job was not available, so I worked in a different part of The Venetian Casino and Resort. I started working as a door attendant. My duties included singing opera tunes to guests, while opening their taxi door and loading luggage when necessary. The job was very lucrative. I enjoyed the work and my newly created life with Laura. The past no longer existed in my mind. I blindly decided to discontinue my prescribed medications after experiencing a rejuvenation of mental health. I became hypomanic within a week. Laura's apartment lacked the presence of furniture, so I decided to remedy the problem. I discovered a used furniture store and found a leather-clad bar with matching stools. I purchased the bar, believing it was exactly what we needed. Laura arrived home to find me sitting at my new acquisition. I was already smoking a cigar and drinking heavily to my success.

Laura flew east the next week, in order to visit her family. I often talked with her on the telephone while she was on the east coast. Things were going well with her family. However, during one of our phone calls I discovered that Laura and her sister were enjoying themselves at a local bar in Baltimore, Maryland. My mind quickly raced with jealousy. I became extremely upset while on the phone. I began to question Laura's sincerity, regarding our relationship. I finished the conversation abruptly and walked to the kitchen utensil drawer.

I was voracious in my efforts to create an outlet for my mind's mental anguish and ever collapsing lucid rational. Thus, I caused a pain, which I could understand. I decided to do so to my face as well while cutting upon my body. I once again cut tattoos. My arms bled heavily with deep penetrating lines across each bicep. I cut my face depicting a design from Native American war paint. The mania I experienced was intense. I allowed the blood to flow freely for a lengthy amount of time. I washed the blood away and peered into the bathroom mirror once I was satisfied with my self-abased artistry. However, I felt the consequences of my wounds immediately. Mania ceased to exist and my mood changed to that of deep depression within seconds of viewing my own reflection.

Laura returned from the east coast a day later. I was wearing a baseball cap when I met her at the airport. I tried to hide my face, because of the shame I felt for what I had done to myself. Laura became very concerned for my sanity. She loved me, but truly discovered there was no way for her to assist my detrimental process of self-destruction. I once again called my mother and father. I told them what I had done to myself. My parents drove from Santa Fe to Las Vegas the following day, due to their unending love for me.

My mother knew how my behavior affected Laura and wanted to talk with her. My parents assured Laura she was not the cause of my cutting. They discovered I had discontinued taking my medications. My parents were extremely disappointed with me. This fact did not improve my waning mental state. Nevertheless, I purchased an airline ticket in order to see my psychiatrist in Santa Fe, New Mexico the next week.

My psychiatrist understood my mental illness well. He said many of his patients often stopped taking their prescribed medications. I ceased to take my medications once I felt stable. I did not fully grasp or comprehend the fact that the medications made this state of mind possible. My psychiatrist increased the dosage of my mood-stabilizer and antidepressant. He asked me to stay on my necessary prescriptions. I flew back to Las Vegas, Nevada a week later and truly realized how much my self-destructive behaviors affected Laura.

Laura no longer wanted to work in Las Vegas, Nevada. I stayed in Las Vegas while she moved to the east coast. Laura became settled and was immediately employed in Maryland. I began to rapid-cycle without her in Las Vegas. I was taking my medications, but they had not yet become therapeutic. I quit my job and returned to New Mexico after a month. I lived in Santa Fe with my parents from October of 2000 until August of 2001. Laura and I kept in touch during that period.

X. End of the Beginning

September 11ᵗʰ, 2001

It was easy to leave Las Vegas, but the fond memories of Laura remained deeply ingrained within my mind. We spoke on the telephone quite often. Laura was doing well in her new career on the east coast. Her success pleased me, but I missed her very much. I visited my psychiatrist every two weeks, explained my depressive thoughts, concerning my tumultuous past, and desire to be with Laura. The fact I was living with my parents greatly affected me as well. My psychiatrist reiterated the importance of my medications. I took my medications as prescribed and my mental health subsequently became more stable.

I called Laura in August of 2001 and asked if joining her in Maryland could be a possibility. She was somewhat resigned, but agreed to see how such circumstances would unfold. My parents bid me farewell in late August of that year and I departed on my motorcycle on route to Maryland. Riding the highways of America was healing. I talked with Laura throughout my trip and was very excited about my arrival back in to her loving arms.

Laura was renting a room in Maryland, but I decided we needed a place of our own. I found a nice guesthouse for rent in Annapolis, Maryland. The room had its own bathroom, but we would have to share the kitchen with the proprietor. Laura and I went together, in order to view the property. She immediately agreed to rent it with me as we gazed through the large window of our room and onto the outlying bay. The view from the bedroom was beautiful. Laura and I moved in the next day and once again became close with one another.

I acted as if Laura had forgotten about my self-destructive behavior in Las Vegas, Nevada. All I allowed myself to remember was the love we shared. The past did not exist for me. This was my base instinct for self-preservation. I had no job or income, but securing employment did not prove difficult for me. I was working as a carpenter within a week. I purchased new tools with my credit card. I travelled to work each morning with my drill and tool belt within the saddlebags of the motorcycle. I strapped my new skill-saw to the passenger seat. The job was simple and tolerated by myself in order to be with Laura. Riding to work was the best part of my day.

However, I experienced vertigo while applying siding panels onto a two-story home during my first week. I became dizzy and disoriented while attaching the siding. I immediately called my psychiatrist and he explained it was a possible side effect of my mood-stabilizer. Thus, needing the job I discontinued my medications. I became disillusioned with my construction job in Maryland within two days without my necessary medications. I quit my job a week later and immediately purchased a New York City actor's trade paper.

I desired to continue with my career as an actor and discovered a suitable audition notice in New York City. The audition date was on Tuesday, September 11th 2001. It was a non-equity audition, so I knew getting to the audition early on, the 11th was imperative. I planned to take the train from Annapolis on September 10th, in order to stay over-night in Manhattan. I rode my motorcycle to the train station in Annapolis on the afternoon of the 10th. An attendant told me motorcycles were not allowed to park in the garage as I entered the parking facility. I could not park elsewhere and was therefore unable to take the train to New York City.

I was angry at the fact my motorcycle was the problem and not the situation. Thus, I rode to the nearest car dealership. I became extremely irrational, but focused on an immediate solution. The only answer I could think of was to sell my motorcycle for a car. A salesperson greeted me as I rode into the first auto dealership I could find. I asked the salesperson if I could trade-in my bike for a car. He said he would be happy to do a trade. The salesperson showed me many vehicles and I quickly chose a black Jeep Wrangler.

I did not look at the quality of the engine, interior, or exterior of the vehicle. My only concern was for an auto with four wheels. I signed the necessary paperwork and said good-bye to my motorcycle as the salesperson handed me the keys to the Jeep. I noticed the hood of my new Jeep was badly tarnished before departing. The salesperson told me to return the next day, where upon a technician would polish the hood. I drove away in my new Jeep, of which I had no idea of the cost. My mind was racing erratically, but I truly believed I had solved my problem.

I stopped at Wal-Mart during the short drive to our home in Annapolis. I was completely disinterested in New York City and the audition while buying new speakers for the Jeep. Laura arrived home to find my new Jeep and me in the driveway. I was installing the speakers when she walked up beside me. I shouted, "I bought a Jeep." Once again, Laura was concerned about my behavior. She entered our residence after a short moment and left me working on the Jeep.

I followed Laura into the house after completing the necessary labor to my new auto's sound system. Laura asked me about my motorcycle while we were eating dinner. I told her I had traded my bike for the Jeep. She knew how much I loved my motorcycle and riding. The bike, which I had customized myself, was gone and I never questioned my rationalization for selling it. I did not look back, and consciously chose to ride the highway of my manic episode instead.

I awoke early on September 11, 2001, and entered the shared kitchen of the home. There was no one else in the house as I searched for something to eat. The owner of the home had left his large plasma television's power on. The television covered a large portion of the wall, and its bright images projected smoke exiting the side of one of the New York City Twin Towers. No sound was coming from the television, so I quietly watched with interest as to what had occurred. I then witnessed a large airplane collide with the other Tower. My mind initially raced upon seeing the Tower explode into fire and debris, but then shattered with disbelief. I immediately realized the severity of the event.

I sat in front of the enormous television and watched the chaos unfold. I needed to hear the comforting voices of my parents, so I called my father. He answered and asked me if I was at my audition in New York City. I told him "no." I could hear his sigh of relief on the other end of the phone. He talked to me for a brief moment and then departed, in order to call Scott who was working in Washington D.C. at the time. As he did so, an image of a destroyed airplane within the exterior walls of the Pentagon filled the large plasma television screen.

I sat for what seemed to be decades. I cried as I witnessed the first Twin Tower crumble and fall. The sight of its total destruction was more than my mind could tolerate. I was continuing to watch as the second Tower collapsed into a million pieces. I crashed with it.

My mind went blank. I wanted to do something which would help someone… anyone. I experienced the emotion of uselessness, due to my inability to contribute. All I could do was watch, while sitting alone in the small home. The indescribable events affected me in a most horrific manner. My life and life itself seemed to have no meaning.

I knew I had to leave the east coast after regaining a minute amount of my ability to rationalize. I ran to my Jeep and drove to the dealership. The same salesperson approached me thinking I had come to have the Jeep's hood repaired. I handed him the keys and told him I could not keep the Jeep. Further, I said I did not care about any loss of capital.

I took a cab to the Annapolis home and Laura soon joined me. We talked at length while listening to the news. Laura and I watched the media replay the tragic event repeatedly. We attempted to find the reasoning behind such destruction. I tried to acquire an airline ticket to Albuquerque, but all flights had been cancelled. I needed my parent's support. I immediately resumed taking my medications, hoping for a miracle. However, the small, colorful pills were unable to immediately accomplish the relief I was requiring.

The relationship I had with my parents was stronger than my relationship with Laura. I left the east coast on the first flight I could acquire from Washington D.C. The flight departed from Reagan National Airport. I viewed the damaged Pentagon building from my window seat as the airplane left the ground. It was a purely sickening site and overwhelmingly ominous to look upon. The reality of what had occurred, on September 11th 2001, greatly affected my mental health. The fact I could not do anything for the thousands who died, caused me to feel completely helpless and useless. I soon after discovered I was helpless... even to myself.

My parents greeted me at the Albuquerque, New Mexico airport. I was relieved to see them. We embraced and then drove to their home in Santa Fe. My psychiatrist met with me the next day. I told him about my deep depression and commented about my need for refills on my medications. He wrote a prescription for a second antidepressant, as well as my mood-stabilizer. I returned home after refilling my prescriptions.

Bipolar, Type I

My depressive mood caused me to sink into despair that night. I could see no possibility of a meaningful future. I hugged my parents and went to bed at nine p.m. I sat on my bed and simply waited for them to fall asleep. I decided to end the chaos myself, with anticipation for a final relief from life's uncontrollable destinies and injustices. I exited my bedroom and entered the guest bathroom. I proceeded to fill a large clear plastic glass with water, which I used to swallow all of my newly refilled prescription medications.

I placed hand full after hand full of my thirty-day prescription of mood-stabilizers into my mouth. The pharmacy had given me sixty 500 mg gray pills. The pills were large and difficult to swallow. I was absolutely determined to end my life however, so I swallowed my thirty-day prescription of both antidepressants as well. My heart was racing as the drugs entered my bloodstream. I left the bathroom and walked back into my bedroom.

I prepared carefully for my last moments on earth. I dressed in a pair of blue jeans, my black cowboy boots, and favorite leather motorcycle jacket. It was difficult for me to write my parents a suicide note. I tried to explain the emotions, which had caused me to self-inflict life's inevitable conclusion. I thanked them for their endless love and signed my name. I lay on my bed after finishing the note and waited for the pills to destroy me. My heart was racing, but my mind went blank.

I only know what occurred thereafter from my father's words. He explained that our dog was barking and woke him at two a.m. My father walked downstairs and heard my boots kicking the door of my closet. He said I was convulsing. My father tried to wake me, but could not. He had no idea as to what was occurring. My father then found my suicide note. He looked in the guest bathroom and discovered my empty prescription bottles. My father immediately called an ambulance. My parents feared I was beyond help.

The ambulance arrived and drove me to the only hospital in Santa Fe. The emergency room doctor pumped my stomach full of a charcoal based liquid. My father held me down as I thrashed about on the emergency room table. The doctor commented it was a good sign that I was able to move. The hospital staff moved me from the emergency room to the intensive care unit, once my stomach was filled with the anti-toxin charcoal. I lay unconscious for eight hours as my father and mother waited by my side. My vital signs improved and I eventually woke. I was confused. I soon became extremely angry as I gained knowledge of where I was. My true desire was for the absoluteness of death.

The doctor entered my hospital room the next day. He explained the mood-stabilizers had not killed me because of their slow absorption into my blood stream as my psychiatrist had prescribed me an extended release dosage. The effect of the drug had not yet produced a great amount of toxicity within my body, even though I had swallowed sixty tablets. The doctor further explained my antidepressants caused the high level of poisoning within my blood steam. This fact did not quell my dissatisfaction and disappointment, however. I truly believed the medications would end my life and many years of mental exhaustion.

Nonetheless, I was respectful to the doctor and hesitantly thanked my parents for saving my life. I had not expected to see the light of the world again. The thought I could not even kill myself correctly was overpowering. I was taken to the psychiatric unit of the same hospital after two days in the intensive care unit. I met with the hospital psychiatrist the first day. He was sincere, but not as effective as my private practice psychiatrist was.

The hospital psychiatric facility did not improve my waning state of mind. I was on medications, but deeply depressed over my failed suicide attempt. The hospital kept me at the psychiatric unit for two weeks. The other patients and I had very few scheduled group meetings, regarding our recovery process. I played board games and ate chocolate pudding during my two weeks in the psychiatric facility. I was still deeply depressed as I left the confines of the hospital.

XI. Psychotic Mixed Episode

Delusional

Returning to my parent's home was extremely difficult for me. I did not know if I could sleep in my room again. I had hoped to die peacefully in my bed less than three weeks earlier. The memory of my overdose forced me to sleep on the living room couch. My parents tried to console me. They explained how relieved they were I had not succeeded with my suicide attempt. I was completely inconsolable, however.

I met with my psychiatrist the week after I returned from the hospital's psychiatric facility. He was very concerned for my mental and physical health. We talked about different medications. My psychiatrist prescribed the same mood-stabilizer, but doubled my dosage. He recommended a different antidepressant and prescribed an anti-psychotic drug. My psychiatrist did so with the hope I would experience no mood-swings or further suicidal ideations. He handed me the new prescriptions and asked me to take them as prescribed. He diagnosed me as bipolar type one, due to my suicide attempt.

Taking my prescribed medications did not relieve me of my deep depression. I decided to cut, in order to relieve my depressive state of mind. I simply waited for my parents to fall asleep and found myself in front of the utensil drawer once again. I grabbed a pair of scissors and walked into my bathroom. I forced the blade deep into my skin and ripped my flesh apart as I stood before the mirror of my bathroom.

I cut furiously and created twenty-four horizontal lines across my torso. I cut a design deep into my chest, similar to that of a Native American Indian warrior chest plate. There were twelve incisions on the left and twelve incisions on the right of my torso. The cuts bled heavily upon my body. The wounds continued to bleed as I washed them with soap. I covered the cuts with paper towels and left them sticking to my torsos abused skin. The blood eventually coagulated.

My manic state of mind soon ceased to exist as I looked into the mirror. I crashed and slept for sixteen hours. I showed my parents what I had done the next day. They were as destroyed as my body. My parents were exhausted by my self- destructive tendencies and immediately insisted I visit my psychiatrist. I made an appointment and was in his office the next day.

My psychiatrist continued to prescribe the same medications as he had the month earlier. He did not want to make any drastic changes and explained to me that my medications only became therapeutic after several weeks. I respected my psychiatrist's professional advice and took my medications. I did not do so for long, however. I stopped taking my mood-stabilizer first. I discontinued all of my medications on December 15th of 2001.

Preparation for my Salvation

I wanted to prove to myself that I could live a normal life. My mind raced out of control after a week without medications, and thus obliterated all rational thought. Eight years of experiencing intense mood-swings was compounded with six years of self-destructive behaviors. I believed the solution to all of my problems lay in my hands. I became delusional beyond a point of no return. I premeditated a concise and well-conceived plan for my salvation.

I walked to the garage where my worm drive circular saw awaited me. I carefully placed my heavy saw into the flimsy walls of a blue nylon sports duffel bag and secretly reentered my parent's home. I placed the colorful package onto the floor of my bedroom closet. I then walked from the closet to my bathroom, where I looked into the mirror and stared at the fresh wounds upon my torso. My mind fought against embracing the images of my self-destruction and I judged myself harshly.

I felt my hands alone had held the blade as I cut. My hands had placed the pills in my mouth as I attempted to commit suicide. My hands had caused the destruction of my body for many years. I believed my hands were the problem. I became immovably determined to end such behaviors while peering deeply into my own reflection. I resolved the only solution was to cut-off my hands.

The circular saw lay caged and hidden in my dark bedroom closet for two days. This fact was not due to any lack of my willful determination, however. My rational reasoning, within my irrational mind chose the date carefully which I would sever my hands from my body. Christmas Eve had always been a very special day in our family. We often enjoyed the festivities at a midnight candle service, or talked together while opening our Christmas presents. Christmas Eve was a night when we withheld no emotions and sincerely cared for one another.

I considered Christmas Eve pure with love, affection, and self-sacrifice. I honestly believed my self-sacrificial action would be just as pure and bring me safely into the future. A life without the ability to harm myself was what I deeply desired. My prescribed medications lay in a drawer not far from my reach, but my fragmented mind never fully grasped the fact they were truly the solution for my health of mind and body.

My brothers Scott and Brad could not join our Christmas celebration in Santa Fe that year. My parents and I decided not to attend a midnight service on Christmas Eve. We watched a film instead and opened a few gifts together. I was soon after fully prepared for my sacrificial act, and told my parents I wanted to retire for the night. We went to our separate rooms shortly thereafter. I merely waited for them to fall asleep. I opened my closet door at eleven thirty p.m. in order to attain my resolute goal. I had the ritual planned to the very last detail. There was no question in my mind as to what I must do and how I was going to accomplish the premeditated task. On the bitterly cold Christmas Eve of 2001, my bipolar disorder finally consumed me.

I gently opened my closet door and relieved my powerful circular saw (4,800 revolutions per minute, which I had previously used to cut lumber in rapid succession) from its blue nylon cage. I slowly exited my bedroom and proceeded to the living room. I set the deadly tool onto the raised ledge of the fireplace and began to prepare my circular saw for its task. I duct-taped the trigger to full throttle, so the crave nous saw would not stop. I taped the cylindrical blade-guard open, until the aggressive silver-colored blade became fully exposed. The blade's vicious teeth where blinding to my distorted retinas.

I pushed the burning coals in the fireplace to left side of the fire pit. The coals were still red with heat and fury. The room was dimly lit, but I could clearly see the power-outlet for the protruding plug of my skill-saw. I plugged the circular saw into the power-outlet at midnight and the blade roared ravenously with a high-pitched scream.

I placed the saw on its back, in order to pull my right arm through the blade. I forcefully pulled my arm through the spinning blade without hesitation. The circular saw cut halfway through my arm. I thrust my arm back into the viciously want nous blade until my right hand was completely severed. The end of my mutilated arm bled profusely, so I pushed my stump into the furious coals of the fire. The sensation was similar to that of ice. The coals cauterized my flesh instantly.

I pulled my stump from the fireplace and found it was no longer bleeding. I made certain my right hand could not be salvaged by throwing it onto the hot coals. The circular saw was still spinning out of control as I prepared to sever my left hand. I heard my father enter the living room and stopped myself from pulling my left arm through the blade. I did so due to the fact I desired my amputation to occur while I was alone. My father frantically unplugged the circular saw and looked at my right arm. He said, "What have you done?" I immediately apologized to my father. "I'm sorry" was all I could think of to say.

My mother had also woken to the loud roar of the circular saw. She entered the living room in her robe and became hysterical while looking at my right arm. My mother screamed "Oh-God" repeatedly. She asked me where my right hand was and I pointed toward the fireplace with my cauterized stump. My mother grabbed my right hand from the coals and went to the freezer. She placed my severed hand into a bucket of ice. My mother looked at me and said, "What are you doing?" I was simply standing in the middle of the room, behaving as if nothing had occurred to my disfigured body. My father asked me to follow him to the car. My mother accompanied us to the garage with my right hand in the bucket of ice.

I entered the rear seat of my parent's vehicle and my mother sat next to me. My father drove us to the hospital in Santa Fe. I remained quite lucid. I could not understand my mother's emotions. My father was driving erratically when I calmly asked him to "please slow down." I looked down at my stump on the way and realized I had succeeded in cutting-off my right hand. My only regret was I had not been given the chance to sever the left hand from my body as well.

We arrived at the hospital, whereupon I slowly entered the two automatic sliding glass doors of the emergency room entrance. A nurse looked at my right arm and asked me to follow her. My parents walked beside me. My mother had calmed herself and was thinking rationally. She handed the nurse my severed hand, still in the bucket of ice. Another nurse had me lay on a bed and told me to stay where I was.

A nurse held white gauze against my stump, even though my arm was no longer bleeding. I looked at my parents and asked for their forgiveness. My father and mother told me that everything would be all right. My parents said they loved me. I looked at them again and apologized for my actions. They repeated their sentiment that they loved me. My mind continued to rationalize I had taken the correct action in severing my right hand.

The shock of my amputation ceased to exist as the nurse continued to hold gauze against my right stump. The wound began to throb intensely. Shock had kept my body from breaking down. It had allowed me to function for hours. My entire being soon after became consumed with the pain of what I had done to my arm. The nurse continued to hold the gauze against my stump as I yelled for her to stop. I screamed at the nurse to give me painkillers, but was administered none.

I was told the hospital was waiting on a physician who could operate on my arm. Hours passed as I waited for the hospital to contact an available doctor. A staff member finally told me a helicopter would be flying me to the University of New Mexico hospital in Albuquerque. She said I would be administered a sedative at my point of departure from the Santa Fe hospital. The wait seemed to take forever. I began to rage at the nurse as she continued to hold gauze against my stump. The pain only increased as she tended to my wound. I called her every hurtful name my delusional and fragmented mind could think of.

The helicopter arrived and I was moved from my room to the roof the Santa Fe hospital. An emergency technician from the University of New Mexico hospital strapped my gurney into the helicopter and administered a sedative medication. She explained it would help me sleep for the helicopter ride to the Albuquerque hospital. We lifted from the black concrete landing area as I lay in the rear of the helicopter. The helicopter was moving unsteadily as we took flight. I passed-out once we were in the air.

A University of New Mexico hospital doctor was sitting at my side when I awoke. He talked to me about possible options for my right arm. The doctor told me he could re-attach my hand, but it was badly burned. Further, he said if I desired to re-attach my right hand it would be four inches shorter than my left, because of the cauterization. He then said they could cut-off the burned portion and stitch-up the wound without my hand. I told him vehemently I did not want my hand to be re-attached. The doctor assured me he would honor my request. It was the most surreal conversation I had ever experienced in my young life.

I woke the next day to find my parents standing beside me in a hospital intensive care unit room. They told me they loved me. I lifted my right arm, in order to see if the doctor had heeded my request, and found my right hand was missing. My right arm had a large cast on the end. I then looked at my parents and whispered I loved them. My mother and father continually told me everything would be all right.

A psychiatrist visited me that day, to attain an assessment of my state of mind. I told her I was fine and I truly was. She was surprised by my candor. I did not tell the psychiatrist I had purposefully severed my hand. I was satisfied with the result of my self-mutilating actions and delightful to the psychiatrist. She did not stay for long. My parents and I talked about my future. I expressed I was optimistic.

I spent three days recovering at the University of New Mexico hospital. Several doctors came to visit me during my last day. The doctor who performed my surgery was in the room. I thanked him for his compassion, concerning my desire to forgo re-attaching my right hand. He asked my permission to donate my right hand for research at the University of New Mexico medical intern program. I told him it would be my honor. The doctors then asked me a few questions. I explained my right hand had been accidentally severed during a late night carpentry task. The doctors signed my discharge paperwork after speaking with me for an hour.

My parents and I drove to Santa Fe after my release from the hospital. I entered the house as if nothing out of the ordinary had occurred in the living room. I simply settled into my new life. I ate meals with my parents, played with our dogs, and slept well at night. I was experiencing a mania the likes of which I had never experienced. I truly had not yet realized the severity of my situation. My psychiatrist wanted to see me the day after my discharge. He talked with me compassionately whilst we were in his office. I confessed to him I had discontinued taking my prescribed medications nine days prior to severing my right hand. My psychiatrist had already come to that conclusion.

I told my psychiatrist every detail about the fateful Christmas Eve. Further, I explained I believed it needed to be done, or I would continue to self-destruct for the remainder of my days on earth. He listened and stated my distorted rationale had been, and was continuing to be caused by a "psychotic mixed episode." My psychiatrist told me the chemistry of my brain was imbalanced and I must remain on medications for the entirety of my life. He further explained medications, along with psychotherapy, were the only solutions for my survival.

XII. The Aftermath

Reality of my Actions

One of my doctors from the University of New Mexico hospital had made an appointment for me to return, in order to remove the cast from my arm. Therefore, my father and I drove to the Albuquerque hospital in early January of 2002. My father stood next to me with a serious expression upon his face as the doctor started to remove the cast. I waited with anticipation, still believing I had taken the correct action in severing my right hand. I looked down at my missing right hand and became uncontrollably emotional.

The end of my arm had many sutures, which were thick and darker than any color of black I had ever witnessed. The doctor proceeded to remove the stitches one-by-one. Several scars revealed themselves. They were hideous to me. The skin was unnaturally joined together and deep purple in color. A strange and extremely painful sensation occurred at the end of my right arm as I looked at the scar tissue. I could feel the entirety of my right hand as if it were still there, and colliding with a brick wall. The doctor explained to me they were "phantom pains." He further explained the phantom sensations would most likely occur throughout the remainder of my life.

I was in a state of shock as my father and I walked back to the car after my appointment was completed. I tried not to reveal my extreme emotions to him. He knew it would be difficult for me to see I was missing my right hand. The mania I had been experiencing and surviving on for many weeks was no longer assisting with my disfigured process. The reality of what I had done consumed me. I could not stop myself from staring at my mutilated appendage, however. The sight of it sickened me and the belief that I had taken the correct action for my salvation, no longer existed. Further, I no longer desired to exist.

I could not bring myself to talk with my father during our drive to Santa Fe. The hour commute seemed endless, due to my absolute self-hatred. I walked into the living room and looked at the fireplace when we arrived back at my parent's home. The memories of Christmas Eve returned to my mind and body. My mind collapsed within seconds of my return to their house and my stump throbbed uncontrollably with pain. Sadness enveloped and consumed my entire being. I turned away from the living room and walked into my bedroom. The memories of my suicide attempt crystallized and overwhelmed me upon entering the bedroom. My immediate reaction was "I can't live here!"

I was devastated and consequently mutated into nothingness. My mind was no longer racing with thoughts of grandiosity. I forced myself to stay in my room and away from the fireplace for the entire day. I took my prescribed medications and slept deeply for sixteen hours. My parents scheduled an appointment for me to see my psychiatrist the following day. My psychiatrist prescribed a new mood-stabilizer and increased the doses of my anti-psychotic, antidepressant, and other mood-stabilizers. His hope was for me to experience no further mood-swings and to quell any further tendencies of mine for self-destructive ideations or behaviors.

I slept sixteen hours per day, because of my many prescribed medications. My parents and I would cry together when I was awake. I had no ability to taste, so food became merely sustenance. My desire for death was all I craved. My incessant ruminations over the gruesome manner in which I severed my own right hand began and would not cease. The horror of my actions consumed my conflicted mind. Vivid memories of the circular saw blade tearing my right hand from its arm flashed through my mind repeatedly. The smell of burning flesh lingered in my sickened nostrils.

I needed a relief from my severe depression and ruminations, so I immediately scheduled an appointment with my psychiatrist. He talked with me about a hospital in Maryland, which specialized in extreme behaviors. My psychiatrist explained the program at the hospital was created for bipolar affective disorder treatment. My psychiatrist said it was a possible beginning for my recovery process.

I left his office with the name and number of the hospital and called for more information later that day. My parents were supportive of my decision to seek further assistance with my mental illness. I scheduled a date to begin receiving treatment after several phone conversations with the facility in Maryland. I left Santa Fe in February of the year 2002.

Therapeutic Love

I arrived at the hospital in Maryland with the desire to learn all I could about my mental illness. It was my hope the hospital would implement an effective plan for my recovery. However, no changes to my existing treatment were recommended after several days. My ruminations only worsened while in the hospital. The other patients and I had very few group sessions during the day. I was not led to learn a solitary helpful aspect of how to survive my mental illness. I found myself sitting in my room all day while losing my mind instead.

I needed the comfort of a friendly voice, so I contacted Laura who was still living in Maryland. She had already learned from a phone conversation with my mother that I purposefully severed my right hand. However, Laura was receptive of my desire to see her, so I asked the doctors for permission to see Laura. I had ritualistically cut-off my own right hand two months earlier, but surprisingly to me the doctors granted a day pass to see Laura. I believed the hospital's lackadaisical candor, regarding my treatment plan to be absurd, but needed to get out of the hospital for a few hours. Laura arrived in front of the hospital at ten a.m. the following day and we enjoyed lunch together. We found ourselves at her new apartment, whereupon Laura and I were intimate with one another.

I could not believe Laura desired me romantically again. My mind pondered as to why and I concluded Laura did not see me as disabled. However, I was very uncomfortable during our lovemaking. I was unable to hold her as I once had in the past. This fact was difficult for me. Laura knew I was insecure and conflicted, but cared for me in the same manner as she always had. Laura truly assisted with my conflicted state of mind that afternoon, regarding my premeditated loss.

Laura drove me back to the Maryland hospital later that evening. I immediately requested another day pass from the doctors when I re-entered the hospital. Laura arrived in front of the facility at ten a.m. again the next day. She and I spent our short time together in the very same manner as we had the previous day. It was wonderful. I had not laughed since September 11th, 2001, but did so during the entire afternoon. I did not feel the overwhelming weight of my disability in Laura's company. She drove me back to the hospital as the sun light of day faded. I kissed Laura goodbye and she departed. My deep depression returned with a vengeance the moment Laura drove away.

I called my parents before my discharge and departure from the hospital. I explained to them I was unable to return to their home in Santa Fe. My parents recommended we move to Tampa, to be closer to my brother Brad. I was thankful for their understanding and agreed upon Florida. The hospital in Maryland helped me in no manner mentally. The only therapeutic process I experienced there was spending two afternoons with Laura. I was no closer to a recovery plan than the month before. I became angry, due to the fact I had sought help and was administered none.

I flew from Maryland to Tampa, Florida and my family met me at the airport. My mother and father asked me about my experience at the hospital and I told them the truth. I explained my afternoons with Laura had been the only real benefit during my stay there. My parents were very disappointed. We had all hoped for some concrete results, concerning my waning mental health and inability to cope with my new disability.

My parents and I looked for a two-bedroom apartment in Tampa and discovered a place near Brad's residence. Living in my own apartment was unthinkable. My mother and father wanted me close to them, so they could possibly provide assistance and keep me safe. I truly needed them for their unending qualities of love and support. We rented the apartment and soon shopped for furniture. My parents purchased couches, beds, a television, and video cassette player. We had a new place to call home within two days. I started to seek employment in Tampa, but had no success in readily finding a job.

The relationship with my parents became strained while living together in the small residence. I was tormented by the action of mutilating my own right arm. I often projected my inner anguish and shouted my self-abasement in my father's direction. He returned my sentiment twice as loud. When my father and I were not fighting, my mother and I were. I was crazed and mad at the world for what I had done to myself. I could not think of one reason to stay in Florida after only three weeks in Tampa. My only real home was our family cabin in New Mexico, so I requested we move there. My parents agreed and we left Tampa a month after arriving.

My parents and I lived at our cabin in the mountains for a year upon our return to New Mexico. My father and I drove to Santa Fe every two weeks, in order for me to meet with my psychiatrist. I told my psychiatrist I was having constant suicidal ideations and explained I could not find one reason to continue living.

The memories of what I had done to my once healthy body haunted me. We talked about my constant ruminations. My psychiatrist and I continued to discuss changing medications, or dosages of the prescriptions I was already taking. I constantly expressed my frustration with the side effects of the medications. My regimen of prescriptions was ever changing that year.

I experimented with twelve different medications during the months of March to December of 2002. I was taking seven medications simultaneously. My medications included antidepressants, mood-stabilizers, and anti-psychotics. My psychiatrist's desire was to keep me safe from myself, hoping to eliminate any extreme mood-swings. We often increased the dosage of my medications. He listened to my intolerance of certain side effects and attempted to discover a helpful combination. I always filled the new prescriptions with hope for my future, or at least relief from my daily mental anguish.

The multitude of medications failed to decrease the depth of my depression, however. I ceaselessly questioned whether I could ever discover hope for a normal life again, due to the purposeful manner in which I had severed my right hand from its natural habitation. My life became excruciatingly intolerable on every occasion I attempted a task which necessitated the use of two hands. In addition, the phantom pains were a constant reminder of December 24th, 2001.

I was utterly consumed by the events of 2001. My entire existence had been obliterated… in the very same manner as the Twin Towers. The only difference was I had no one else to blame other than myself. I became extremely angry and resentful with my bipolar disorder. Looking upon my own reflection in the mirror was mentally disabling. Hopelessness and constant ruminations enveloped my entire being.

My parents and I cried as we attempted to play cards on Christmas Eve of 2002. We were at our cabin and far away from the fireplace in Santa Fe. However, no matter how great a distance I placed between me and my parent's home in Santa Fe, my missing right hand was still the most excruciating reminder of the horrific events that occurred in 2001. My self-destructive past, conflicted present, and unknown future, haunted every crevasse of my unstable mind.

Hell

My parents and I decided to move back to their Santa Fe home in January of 2003. I agreed to the relocation, believing I could overcome my fears. However, the house proved to be very difficult for me to live in and my suicidal ideations only increased with every passing hour while surrounded by its haunting memories. I visited my psychiatrist as soon as I was able. He continued to prescribe four of my medications, but discontinued three. My psychiatrist replaced the three with three new medications. We increased the dosage of each medication every few months thereafter. I always attempted to remain hopeful with the changes. Again, I was taking seven medications simultaneously.

I believed my self-destructive thoughts would decrease if I covered my stump, so my parents helped me to purchase a prosthetic. Gainful employment was a goal of mine as well. Hanger Prosthetics in Santa Fe created a plastic prosthetic to fit over my right arm. I had asked him to make the prosthetic black...the very color of my uncontrollably debilitating moods. The technician recommended a useful attachment for a hand. The attachment was a stainless steel claw, which I found difficult to practically function.

The prosthetic was uncomfortable. This fact did not alter my desire to cover my missing hand, however. I wore the prosthetic whenever in public, because of my inner shame and desire to cover my hideous stump. The emotions, which I experienced when people stared at my right arm, were overwhelming. I hated myself deeply as strangers looked for long moments upon my prosthetic. Further, I despised what I referred to as the "perfectly whole-bodied person!" My mind created this term and image to include everyone who did not have a physical disability.

I found a small amount of peace in my bedroom and slept most of the day and night. I was completely introverted and did not care to meet with old acquaintances or make new ones. My parents tried to show me life had many possibilities, but I was mentally withdrawn and inconsolable. I did not believe any aspect of life could bring me contentment, let alone happiness, ever again. The pain and suffering of the world was upon me, similar to the story of *Sweeney Todd*. I realized my life had been filled with beautiful music, but my own self-destruction had caused me to hear only the dissonance of life's tumultuous soundtrack.

My mother was diagnosed with breast cancer in July of 2003. The depth of my depression caused me to sink even further into the bowels of hell with her diagnosis. My mother was extremely strong, regarding her fate. She battled her illness selflessly. She was very worried for my safety and further explained the cancer did not concern her.

My mother was diagnosed with cancer again that year and fought the lengthy battle with chemotherapy and radiation treatments. Somehow, she retained her unwavering positive attitude. My mother explained her illness was no different from my bipolar disorder. Her illness deeply affected me, however. In my mind, life had become even more pointless and futile.

My parents were always in the house with me. My mother took the knives and scissors from the utensil drawer and placed them in her locked closet. My father cleared the garage of all power tools and threw them into the garbage dumpster of a local grocery store. My medications were in a locked box and administered to me every morning and night. My father disengaged the power to the kitchen garbage disposal when I told my parents I was going to destroy my left hand within it. My mother went as far as to hide the blender and toxic cleaners from me.

My parents wanted to keep me safe from myself and alive. I knew they did these things because they loved me, but was angry due to my need for assistance. I lacked the self-control to keep myself safe, so I left it up to my parents to do so. My mother and father told me they lay in bed every night listening and waiting for the high-pitched scream of the circular saw. They hoped the sound would never resonate in their home again. Something deep inside of me desired the powerfully destructive saw, or at least a pair of scissors.

I talked about the loss of my right hand incessantly with my mother and father. My parents understood my need to talk through the past, but doing so only caused my mother a great deal of anguish. Discussing the past was unhealthy for me as well. I could not stop ruminating about my self-mutilation and many years of self-destruction, however. I was trapped in a vicious cycle, which I perpetuated myself.

My existence was filled with nothing but the horrific destruction that had occurred to right my hand… by my own hand. Every recollection caused me to relive the events of 2001. I constantly reflected upon September 11th, 2001, suicide, cutting my body, and finally the severing of my own hand. My mind played-out the images and consequences repeatedly. I was consumed with the thousands of victims, taking the pills, cutting, and forcing my hand back through the vicious circular saw. My parents told me I was creating my own individual hell. I was in hell… burning with rage for what seemed to be an eternity.

XIII. Incessant Inquiries

"What Happened to your Hand?"

Laura called me from Maryland in July of 2003 and asked permission to visit me in Santa Fe. She also desired to see an opera at the Santa Fe Opera House. I agreed and Laura arrived in late August. We went to see *The Marriage of Figaro*. My parents joined Laura and me for dinner before the opera. I ordered the grilled lobster. I was wearing my black prosthetic that night. I proceeded to try to cut the tender meat once the food had arrived. My parents and Laura asked if I needed help. I became perturbed and was too prideful, so stringently declined. I needed to prove to myself I was able bodied and self-sufficient.

I attempted to grasp the fork with my prosthetic claw while holding the knife in my left hand. The fork would not remain within my claw's grasp, however. I was relentless and did my best for thirty-minutes until my meal became cold. I finally grabbed the lobster with my left hand and shoved the meat into my mouth. The melted butter was all over my hands and face, but I succeeded in my goal to be self-reliant. The other patrons looked distastefully upon my manners. I did not care. I needed to eat the meal solely of my own accord.

The four of us headed to the Opera after my frustrating bout with dinner. We all had wine at the restaurant and I continued to do so at the Santa Fe Opera House. I drank heavily and became hypomanic while singing the Italian ballad *Sorrento* from the third balcony of the opera house's outer deck before the opera began. The lead usher quickly approached and told me to stop. I had already finished the aria and re-joined Laura, after having accomplished my aspiration of singing at the Santa Fe Opera.

We all enjoyed the opera that night, regardless of my drunken state. Laura flew back to Maryland the next day. My mania ceased with her departure and absence in my life. I never spoke to Laura or saw her again, as per her final request. Her words crushed all hope within me of ever loving again.

My psychiatrist discontinued to prescribe my anti-psychotic medications in December of 2003. He maintained my two antidepressants and three mood-stabilizers, however. We continued to change the dosages of each medication on a regular basis. The mood-stabilizers seemed to be helpful with my mood changes as long as I was not drinking vast amounts of alcohol. My mental health was steadily improving. However, my family's attempt to celebrate Christmas proved to be increasingly difficult.

I was determined to live a normal life, so I decided to seek employment after the holiday season. I discovered a job notification for the Santa Fe Ski Area while looking through the local paper in January of 2004. They were hiring for seasonal employees. Most of the jobs required the use of two hands however. Nonetheless, I completed an employment application. I was on the mountain working as a ski-lift operator two weeks later. Initially, the job proved to be very difficult while working with only my left hand. I quickly learned to compensate and within a week was swinging the heavy metal chairs for the patrons with ease.

Working as a lift operator improved my spirits for a brief period. The outdoors calmed my mind. I tried not to think about my disability. This proved impossible, however I was constantly confronted by stranger's inquiries and the inevitable question "what happened to your hand?" My mind and body always became consumed with the event of December 24th, 2001, upon hearing the painful question. One minute I was content in my job and the next moment I hated myself. *I did not want to explain the most horrific moment in my life with a complete stranger!* The curiosity of a child was one thing, but I believed an adult would have more tact than to ask such a personal question. Further, I despised people for their blatant disregard of my personal privacy and disability. I became irritated and inwardly angry toward my inquisitors as the winter ski season progressed.

I always enjoyed being in the spotlight during my career as an actor, but after 2001 I truly desired to be anonymous. I was continually reminded of the fact I was disabled. My mood changed during working hours and I was deeply affected by unrelenting questions about my missing right hand. I created a false story after realizing people were never going to stop asking, "What happened to your hand." I began telling people I lost my hand in a carpentry accident and incorporated some truth within my necessity to lie.

I explained, "My circular saw kicked-back while building a table for my father. I looked down and my hand was lying on the floor… severed. Therefore, I grabbed my right hand, with my left and entered the house, where upon I cauterized my stump in the hot coals of the fire that my parents had been enjoying during the cold evening. My parents drove me to the hospital in Santa Fe, but they could do nothing for me. A helicopter from Albuquerque flew me to the University of New Mexico hospital. Somehow, my right hand ended up in the fire and thus the doctors could not re-attach it. I lost my hand on Christmas Eve."

I started to believe the story myself. It was a heroic tale. I knew telling the truth would make people uncomfortable and cause them to judge me harshly. I had already judged myself harshly, considering my self-mutilating act. The truth never exited my mouth. Further, I never told anyone about my bipolar disorder. I wanted people to see the strength in me, instead of the weakness. Most people focused on the fact I had the wherewithal to stop the bleeding by cauterizing the wound. I disliked telling the lie, but my self-hatred was briefly displaced by keeping the horrific truth to myself.

The Ski Area was the starting point, concerning my ability to convincingly lie. I began to tell untruths with ease. Lying gained in frequency within my life, after proclaiming the carpentry story about my severed hand. I even started to lie to my family. My parents believed my moods were improving. However, during a day free from work I purchased a pair of scissors and started cutting upon my body again. I re-opened the wounds I had previously cut upon my torso. The cuts bled heavily and I felt the same momentary relief from my depression as I had throughout my past.

I broke my prosthetic after a month of working at the SF ski area. The claw was not affected, but the arm was shattered. I quit the job immediately. I was unable to tolerate the endless questions concerning my stump and missing hand. The prosthetic provided me with a certain amount of security. I felt truly vulnerable and exposed once it was no longer functional.

My parents and I decided to invest in a stronger prosthetic material. The manufacturer of my claw recommended a prosthetics company in Colorado Springs, Colorado. I scheduled an appointment with Abilities Unlimited after discarding my old prosthetic. The name of the company was inspiring to me. I did not believe my disability had unlimited potential as an ability.

Abilities Unlimited was a five-hour drive from Santa Fe. My parents and I drove to Colorado Springs for my initial measurements. The technician said I needed two more fittings after completing the initial process. The technician showed me two different color options for my prosthetic during the second session. The choices he gave me were tan or black. I chose black of course.

I received my new prosthetic a month after my first measurements were recorded. It was constructed of black carbon fiber. The technician told me the material was not likely to shatter. I was not so much concerned about the durability, due to my enumeration with the black and gray-checkered pattern of the carbon fiber. I needed to cover my stump in order to hide my secret and it was a most ominous solution. I placed the prosthetic on my arm and it fit well.

The technician then showed me how to wear the silicon glove on my stump, in order for the prosthetic to stay on my arm. The glove was restricting and decreased the blood circulation to the end of my right arm. My phantom pains increased as well while wearing the silicon glove and prosthetic. However, I was determined to appear more socially acceptable, so I attached my claw into the prosthetic while the technician connected the necessary cable and harness. He showed me how the voluntary-close hand mechanism operated and I was content with the finished product.

I was ready for employment opportunities after the purchase of my new prosthetic. I applied and was hired at a clothing store. I was employed as a sales associate, but the job proved to be challenging. The sales aspect was not difficult for me, but folding the clothing items proved to be impossible. I did my best, but eventually resigned from my position because of patrons endless inquiries as to my missing right hand. My mood always changed whenever confronted with the personally intimate nature of my disability. The relationship with colleagues, and managers, was also affected by my mood swings. I understood the severity of my bipolar disorder and began to believe maintaining a job was to be impossible.

A Much needed Romance

I often visited the local movie theater during my many months of unemployment. I entered the theatre in Santa Fe on one occasion, whereupon a woman gave me a compliment on my prosthetic. I was flattered and asked if sitting with her during the movie might be a possibility. She agreed to my request and we sat one seat apart in the back of theater. The woman was mesmerized with the film. She mesmerized me. She had streaks of pink highlights throughout her blonde hair. It was different and beautiful. The film was extremely violent, and many of the characters had their limbs severed by a samurai sword. I became deeply disturbed by the movie, but the compelling presence of the woman kept me in my seat.

The film finally ended and, as we exited the theater together, the woman asked me what my plans were for that evening. I replied I had nothing to do. The woman asked me if I wanted to join her at a local bar later that night. I said it would be my pleasure. I asked for her name and she told me it was "Iris." "A beautiful name, for a beautiful girl" I thought to myself. I told her my name in return and we parted ways.

I was nervous about spending time with Iris that evening. I had not been with a woman romantically, besides Laura, since the loss of my right hand. Nonetheless, I dressed and drove to the pub. I arrived earlier than our appointed time and ordered a beer. Iris soon joined me and we had a drink while discussing the film we had viewed earlier in the day.

Iris soon asked if I wanted to join her for a beer at her home. I had grown comfortable with Iris during our playful conversation during the evening and replied I would love to. Iris soon after asked the inevitable question, so I divulged the details of my carpentry accident. She thought I was brave, but I disliked lying to my new friend. Iris kissed me and I kissed her in return. We were intimate with each other that night.

I had only known Iris for an afternoon, but allowed myself to embrace her passion. I needed a young woman to desire me physically. My void of self-worth was temporarily filled by our lovemaking. I was more than aware of my disability, but felt I was once again desirable to the opposite sex. I kept my prosthetic on during our intimate encounter. I was still very ashamed of my stump.

Iris and I started to date. She was content with my vibrant personality until she discovered my true disability… my mind. I was taking my prescribed medications, but experienced mood-swings during our relationship. Iris and I drank alcohol together and my initial reaction was hypomania. Depression entered into our relationship as my drinking increased in volume. Iris was unable to tolerate my illness, as was I.

XIV. Normalcy?

The Hand

I decided to remain unemployed as the 2004 Christmas holiday season approached. I asked my parents if we could spend Christmas Eve with my brother Brad in Tampa, to be far from the memories in Santa Fe. My mother and father agreed upon my request. They believed, as did I, being in their home for the holidays would possibly cause a reoccurrence of my self-destructive behaviors. My father purchased airline tickets for our family to arrive in Tampa on the 17th of December.

Brad greeted us at the Tampa airport when we arrived. Brad's family accompanied my parents and I to Busch Gardens the next day. I rode the new roller coasters with my ten-year-old nephew, and we were both thrilled by the rides. We all enjoyed Busch Gardens the following day as well. The days passed quickly, but my mind grew unable to distract itself from the looming inevitability of December 24th.

We all ate dinner together at our favorite restaurant on Christmas Eve. I drank a few beers during my meal, but wanted to drink much more. My parents went back to their hotel room after we had all finished eating. Brad and I departed to his home and on route; I requested we stop at a liquor store for some beer. I purchased a twelve pack of cheap beer at a nearby supermarket.

Brad and I drank a beer together once at his house. Brad then left me in the living room as he prepared his children's clothes for Midnight Mass that evening. I proceeded to get drunk while sitting alone with the memories of Christmas Eve 2001 still burning within my mind. I drank a further ten more beers between nine thirty, and ten p.m. Brad had four beers in his refrigerator, so I drank those as well. My self-destructive actions of 2001 faded somewhat from memory while becoming extremely intoxicated.

The Midnight Mass started at twelve a.m., but we all arrived at the Catholic Church at eleven thirty p.m. It was quiet in the Church. I was drunk and the religious ceremony kept me from enjoying the high. Sitting in my seat was the only task that I was able to accomplish during the service. Further, the Catholic priest continually asked the congregation to rise to their feet. Standing was difficult for me. In addition, the congregation often sang religious prayers that I was unfamiliar with. The midnight mass became a hindrance, regarding my altered state of mind and desire to consume more alcohol. It truly was not a religious experience for me.

Every other person in the large sanctuary seemed to be moved by the ceremony. I was annoyed and growing more angry at every passing moment. God was far from my mind that night, as he had been for many years. I was angry with God, the world, and myself. I also despised the beautiful people during the service. I believed everyone was more beautiful than me, because of his or her whole bodies. The young people, with all of life's possibilities ahead of them, made me mentally sick. I wanted to start my life over again, believing a clean slate might rid me of my inner anguish and pain. I knew this dream to be impossible and thus believed life to be pointless and futile once again.

My parents and I departed from Tampa early on Christmas day. I was terribly hung-over. My mother and father were very disappointed with my drinking of alcohol the night before. I did not care what opinion my family had of me, however. As far as I was concerned, the 24th of December would be my day to behave as I pleased. If getting intoxicated rid me of my memories for a few hours, then that is what I would do. I planned to get drunk every Christmas Eve until exhaling my last breath on earth.

I received a letter from Hanger Prosthetics in Santa Fe after returning from the debacle of Christmas Eve in Tampa. They believed I was still wearing the prosthetic they had crafted for me. Hanger Prosthetics wanted to make an appointment to discover whether it still fit well. I reluctantly made an appointment and visited their office a day later. I entered the technician's office and told him the plastic prosthetic had shattered. I showed him my new carbon fiber prosthetic and he commented positively on the work Abilities Unlimited had accomplished.

I was unsatisfied with the claw attachment however, so asked the technician if there were any "real" looking hands available for my new prosthetic. He commented he had a manufacturer's catalogue full of different attachments. I viewed some interesting options as we looked through the large binder. The technician flipped through the last few pages and, as he did so, a prosthetic hand caught my eye. I thought it was beautiful and requested he order the hand for me. The technician called a week later to inform me my new hand was at his office. I immediately drove to Hanger Prosthetics and he greeted me with a smile.

The fingers of the hand opened voluntarily. I placed the harness around my left shoulder, which had a cable leading to the prosthetic. The cable was then attached to my new hand. The hand opened as I extended my right arm and closed as I retracted it. The technology was simple, but necessary for my level of comfort when meeting new people.

Firmly shaking the hand of another person was a sign of respect as the son of a military man. I truly despised meeting new people after the loss of my right hand. When people would introduce themselves, they would inevitably extend their right hand in order to shake mine. All I manage to do was to extend my left hand in return. The person and I always had an uncomfortable moment shaking hands in this manner. I became more confident when greeting people after the purchase of my new prosthetic hand.

Further, the fingers were crafted of silver metal springs. I loved the shine they produced, and contrast to the black color of the carbon fiber. The material for the hand was tan, hardened plastic. The fingertips were tan rubber. I knew what finishing touches would be necessary before leaving the technician's office. The tan color of the hand had to be altered.

A shopping mall near my parent's home had a leather-goods retailer, so I headed there after leaving Hanger Prosthetics. I arrived at the leather shop and inquired as to their selection of black leather right-handed gloves. The owner looked at my prosthetic hand and asked if the glove was to be worn on it. I replied it was and she walked into the store stock room. The owner re-appeared holding a box with several gloves to choose from. She said to take whichever one pleased me. I found a stylish black glove while feverishly sifting through the box. The glove fit perfectly upon my right prosthetic hand.

I became hypomanic, due to my exhilaration over the new hand. I immediately asked my mother for a pair of scissors after arriving home. She hesitated and asked me why I needed scissors. My parents were still very concerned for my safety. I showed her my new hand and explained its necessity for some improvements. My mother reluctantly handed me a pair of scissors. I quickly walked downstairs to work on my new project and proceeded to make my entire right arm completely black, except for the silver fingers.

I removed the finger portions of the leather glove with the scissors. My alteration covered the tan portion of the hand. The black leather contrast against the silver fingers created a very ominous appearance. The only tan color remaining was the rubber fingertips, so I removed the black dye from my shoe polishing kit and painted the fingertips black. I embraced my creation with great pride after completing the necessary alterations.

My new acquisition provided me much more confidence in my appearance. I loved my uniquely sinister black prosthetic. I felt proud to wear it in public. People would still stare at my prosthetic, but this fact no longer affected me in the same manner as it had in the past. I convinced myself it was acceptable to be different. The depression I had previously been experiencing subsided for a brief amount of time while hypomanic about my newly crafted right arm.

I gained a healthier view on life and sought employment once again. I often shopped at a consignment store near the downtown area of Santa Fe and decided to ask the owner if she needed any assistance. The owner soon hired me and I began selling used clothing. The job did not entail a great amount of physical effort. The shop's clothing usually hung from hangers, so I did not have a great amount of folding to accomplish. It was my hope others would witness and compliment me on my prosthetics beauty. I was experiencing a respite from depression after starting the job, but found strangers continued to only ask about my physical disability.

Once again, I began to be questioned constantly about my missing right hand. A deep depressive mood always followed when asked, "What happened to your hand?" My severe mood-swings began to re-occur while working at the consignment store. This fact was compounded by wearing my prosthetic for eight hours a day. The prosthetic became terribly uncomfortable after a few hours into my shift and the phantom pains always increased my level of anxiety.

I always returned home after work and immediately removed my prosthetic. I was physically most comfortable without the prosthetic. Mentally however, I needed my prosthetic to disguise the truth and cover my stump. I truly believed my body appeared deformed without my right hand. In the guest bathroom of my parent's house hung a large mirror. The bathroom mirror always caused me to suffer a great amount of depression. I truly hated my own reflection and believed my stump to be hideous. Ruminations always followed as the mirror reminded me of my own self-mutilation. Mental exhaustion followed soon thereafter.

My disfigured reflection further compounded my unstable mental health with self-hate. The phantom pains I felt daily, as well, intensified my depression. I experienced the intense emotions of my loss constantly. The owner of the consignment shop witnessed my drastic mood-swings and often talked with me, regarding my behavior with patrons and colleagues. I was not fired, but quit the job after only two months.

Lying

I continued to meet with my psychiatrist every two weeks. He prescribed many medications with the hope I would cease to have self-destructive ideations. There was truly no other solution to the severity of my bipolar disorder. I had experienced twelve years of mood swings without medications and nearly destroyed myself while regulating or discontinuing my prescriptions. I had no choice but to take medications after the events of Christmas Eve of 2001. I had to live with them or die without them.

My psychiatrist decided in January of 2005 to maintain the medications I had been taking throughout 2004. I was on two antidepressants and three mood-stabilizers. My willingness to continue taking the medications was successful in suppressing my self-destructive behaviors. The medications were effective, but not perfect. I was still experiencing severe depression, but never followed through with any suicidal ideations.

I did not like taking my prescribed medications, however. Every dose reminded me of my mental illness. My parents lived in constant fear for my safety. My deep depression and self-destruction greatly affected my family. My mother and father witnessed my actions, but possessed no ability to keep me from harm, since I was reluctant to remain medicated. They trusted me and hoped I could discover the will to live.

My parents attempted to assist me in every way they could and often tried to give me advice about my life. I reacted to their suggestions as if they were a condemnation and often threatened suicide in return to what they referred to as "tough love." I truly believed if my parents did not love me, then nobody would. I knew my desire for their complacency and unconditional support to be completely self-centered. I was not properly caring for my mental illness and thus placed the burden upon my parent's shoulders.

My parents had to live with the consequences of my actions, as well as myself. They knew I no longer cared to live. They never ceased in their attempts to help me discover a solitary reason to live, however. My mother and father always believed the worst was behind me when I would experience a brief respite from depression. Their desire for my stability and improving state of mental health was often crushed, but my parents never gave up hope. My mother often requested I find something to occupy my time, so I again researched gainful employment.

I secured employment with ResCare, Northern New Mexico in March of 2005. ResCare was a company, which operated residences for disabled individuals. I was hired as a Residential Services Manager. My job entailed supervising the direct care staff of three disabled men in their Santa Fe home. Their ages ranged from seventeen to sixty. Two of the men had the necessity of a wheelchair. I understood how it felt to be physically disabled and performed my duties with a dedication to their daily comfort.

I cooked my favorite chili dish for the men during my first evening as their Residential Services Manager. The sixty year old man desired to have a beer with my chili, so I purchased him one while shopping for the necessary groceries earlier that the day. He had not had a beer in many years and became quite tipsy. His wheelchair was motorized and I learned how powerful it was later that night. He raced down the long hall after dinner and tried to turn into the kitchen. Two of the four wheels on his chair lifted from the ground as he turned. He laughed boisterously after the chair corrected itself. I laughed with him. His smile and facial expression was one of complete contentment.

There was a great amount of paperwork involved while working with ResCare. Writing with my left hand was difficult and I struggled with it constantly. In addition, trying to write left-handed always reminded me of what I had done to myself. I used my father's laptop computer to complete the necessary paperwork instead. My first attempt at typing proved to be difficult, but at least the ResCare personnel could understand my legible reports. I became proficient within a few days of teaching myself to type one-handed and enjoyed the quiet evenings, while working on my new computer in men's company.

The older man loved motorcycles. He had several motorcycle logo stickers on the back of his wheelchair. I asked him if he was interested in decorating his wheelchair, after recalling I still had some chrome motorcycle parts in the garage of my parent's home. His eyes smiled with anticipation. I arrived with chrome parts the next day and attached them to his chair with speaker wire. He was grateful and said the new additions looked "cool." I received a great amount of joy from the three men. I did my best to provide them with a comfortable and safe home. I truly believed their physical disabilities were more challenging than my own and treated them with a great amount of respect.

My joy ended abruptly after only a few months with ResCare, due to poor life choices once again. A friend and I were drinking beer at a local tavern, with a few other people on a cool spring Santa Fe April afternoon. We finished our drinks and she invited us all to continue the party at her house. I liked the woman and she knew it. There were four of us at her house. My friend proceeded to ask if I minded that she and the others used some cocaine. I said I would like to try some as well, because of my romantic inclination for her.

We free-based cocaine for six hours. My heart was racing and so was my mind. I became high with my friend, hoping she would approve of me romantically. I was a fool and manic, due to the cocaine. I was afraid my medications would react badly with the cocaine, so I did not take my prescriptions the next morning. My rational mind ceased to exist within twenty-four hours of getting high on cocaine and I experienced a rapid-cycling mixed episode of manic depression. I became deluded and my complete self-destructive desire was once again upon me. I decided to leave the country as soon I possibly could, in order to kill myself overseas.

I was completely disappointed with myself. The reckless decision to do drugs truly exacerbated my already waning mental state. My desire to die, in order to spare myself further self-hatred, became the only conclusion my unhealthy mind could think of. Further, I believed it would cause my parents less pain if they were not the unfortunate souls to discover my lifeless body.

My mind raced as I started to think of ways I could leave Santa Fe without alarming my mother and father. The deep recesses of my delusional mind began to create an intricate lie. I decided writing a phony film screenplay would surely get me out of the country. I immediately started to type on my computer. My concept was of a horror film about WWI and Prince Ferdinand. The screenplay was a mess. I tried to explain the storyline to my parents and they surprisingly thought it had potential.

My father decided he would assist me and searched the internet for material about WWI and the assassination of Arch Duke Ferdinand of Austria. He printed thirty pages of history for me. A descent story, with an interesting twist evolved in my mind as I read the materials. I truly believed I had a good, though falsely created screenplay, after several days of typing on my computer. I approached my parents soon after telling the extravagant lie and told them I had submitted a rough draft to a producer in Los Angeles. Further, I said he wanted to make a film of my screenplay.

I told my parents the producer desired to meet me in person. I explained he wanted to "collaborate" with me and I would be in Los Angeles for a week. My parents were excited for me. They witnessed my efforts while working on the screenplay and believed it had potential for success. My parents had a great amount of trust in me, and they were hopeful I was gaining stability, regarding my mental health. My mother and father were unaware my mind had already departed and I had created the lie so I may simply say "good-bye."

XV. Sinking Further

Credit Card Debt

I often received checks in the mail from my credit card companies to be used as cash. I had two such checks in my dresser drawer. I cashed one of the $10,000 checks after starting the lie about my screenplay. The money went into my bank account the next business day. I decided to invest a portion of the money in a new tattoo, as well as an airline ticket.

I was disgusted with the appearance of my stump, so I decided to cover the scars on the end of my right arm. I proceeded to a local Santa Fe tattoo parlor in May of 2005 to make the end of my right arm look more presentable. I told the artist I wanted a tattoo of a bear claw on my stump. I desired the particular design due to its symbolism and with respect for my family heritage.

My late uncle Robert Lawson Little was a forest ranger in the Grand Canyon. He loved to eat rattlesnake meat. The vertebrae of the snake fascinated my uncle, so he burned the remaining flesh from the vertebra after consuming the meat and collected them. Another ranger asked my uncle if he wanted to trade a few bear claws for some snake vertebra. They exchanged items and, before passing away from Hodgkin's disease, my uncle gave me one of his bear claws. He told me it was a symbol of "power and protection." I kept the bear claw in my possession for twenty-five years, while reflecting upon my uncle's gracious spirit.

The tattoo artist explained a solitary bear claw would not look very appealing, so he sketched a tribal style bear paw with claws on the end of my stump. The paw covered my scars and the bear claws wrapped upward toward my forearm. The artist began to tattoo the end of my right arm once he and I were both satisfied with the sketch. The pain was intense while the artist forced the black ink into my skin. My hypomania gained momentum as the artist tattooed over the two bones at the end of my stump.

The ink would not readily penetrate the scar tissue, so the artist increased the size of the tattooing needle. My arm was bleeding heavily, especially at the end. The tattoo artist wiped the blood away every few seconds while pressing down on the needle. He finished my new tattoo in two hours. The artist accomplished his task and my stump was covered with a beautiful work of art. I truly believed I would finally feel more comfortable in the judgmental public eye without wearing my prosthetic.

I left the tattoo parlor in a complete state of mania and decided to join the ensuing frivolity at a local bar. I walked into the bar and ordered a beer. I felt high on life as I carried my beer to an outside table and began to drink. I was not wearing my prosthetic for the first time in public. The bear claws created a sense of both power and protection within me. I felt the bear paw replaced my missing hand. I desired for others to stare at my right arm, in order to realize its true beauty.

I began to think of where I would travel after finishing my phony screenplay. I chose Australia as the final destination of my life. I initially thought of going to Japan, where I had previously lived with my parents during my high school education. However, I decided against the idea because of the language barrier. I packed my suitcase and was ready for the end of my future.

I knew my father would pursue my where a bouts if I disappeared from the face of the planet. He would visit all of the travel agencies in Santa Fe to discover where I had gone. Thus, I decided to fly to Las Vegas, Nevada, in order to purchase my airline ticket to Australia. I immediately booked a round-trip ticket to Las Vegas. I explained to my parents I was going to visit an old friend, but would return to Santa Fe before my meeting with the producer in Los Angeles. I flew to Las Vegas the next day. I found a reliable travel agent within an hour of arriving and procured my airline ticket to Sydney Australia. I was more than pleased with my crafty plan and proceeded to get drunk at Caesar's Palace.

I danced for many hours and then drove my rental car to the nearest striptease club, where I continued with my intoxicating behavior until the sun was rising over the Nevada desert. I headed back to the airport at six a.m. A police cruiser on route stopped me, as I was driving very recklessly. The police officer's drew their guns and shouted for me to exit my vehicle. I did not have a shirt on as I stepped out of the car and the officers noticed the many scars upon my chest and arms. They questioned me about the wounds and I responded I was bipolar. The officers then lowered their weapons and proceeded to write me several traffic tickets.

The police officers impounded my rental car, but did not arrest me. I was given my well-deserved citations and stringently told to take a taxi to the airport. I was still intoxicated when I flew back to Santa Fe, New Mexico later that day. The cost of the traffic tickets, combined with my impounded rental car was $1,110.

Australia

I spent a few days in Santa Fe after returning from Las Vegas and prepared for my overseas travels. My parents drove me to the airport and wished me luck on the day of my departure. The reality of my lie was painful when they said "good-bye." The thought I would never see them again hurt deeply. I was determined nonetheless. I flew from Albuquerque to Los Angeles and then to Sydney, Australia. The flight cost me two-thousand dollars. The price included a return ticket that I did not plan on using. I was unable to sleep during the sixteen-hour flight, so I enjoyed myself as I drank the free beer from Los Angeles to Sydney.

The flight arrived in the early morning hours of May 13th, 2005. I took a cab to a nice hotel in downtown Sydney. I owned only one suitcase full of clothes and six-thousand dollars. It was nine a.m. when I checked into the hotel. I unpacked and was in the hotel lobby fifteen minutes later. I asked the desk clerk where I could purchase an alcoholic beverage and he pointed to the pub across the street. I walked into the pub and ordered a beer.

The bartender told me about a rugby match occurring later that evening. I headed to a local sporting events shop, after finishing my drink. I was determined to enjoy my last few days on earth, so I purchased a ticket for the match and then walked to the Sydney Opera House. I sat at a little café near the opera house and drank several beers while gazing at the beautiful scenery surrounding me. The beauty was no match for my inner beast, however.

I was manic in my desire to leave the United States, but became deeply depressed once in Australia without my prescribed medications. I self-medicated by drinking alcohol all day and night. My constant intake of alcohol did not cease for ten days. I spent every day drinking beer in my hotel room. My intoxicated evenings were spent in the red-light district of Sydney. I danced in the many nightclubs and attempted to enjoy myself. I created many new and more interesting lies when questioned by the locals about my missing right hand. They were dually impressed with the untruths I was espousing.

I found I desired a different location in which to destroy myself after ten days in Sydney. The hotel clerk told me I should visit the Great Barrier Reef. I packed my suitcase without hesitation and flew to Cannes, Australia later that afternoon. I took a bus to my hotel once there. It was in a very quaint village close to the Reef. My room was beautiful and the perfect place to end my life. However, I could not decide on how to perform my suicide.

I spent a week thinking of a solution to my problem. I was able to distract myself from mental anguish by drinking beer at the many restaurants in the area. I occupied most of my time drinking alcohol with an Australian couple that I had met in one of the restaurants. The woman was gorgeous. I became distraught, because of my inability to end my life abruptly, so I decided to stay in Australia. Thus, I asked the woman if she would marry me while enjoying my new friends and plenty of alcohol one evening. The man understood my desire to marry his girlfriend, but wanted to marry her himself. I was embarrassed, so I departed from their company and continued to drink alcohol in my hotel room.

I soon after flew back to Sydney, where my return ticket to the United States awaited me. I decided to use the return ticket and travel home. I was mentally exhausted by self-destructive ideations and daily intoxication. I arrived in Sydney and left Australia in a blurry haze of discontent for my inability to accomplish my conquest for a relief from life's inevitable transition to nothingness.

XVI. A Necessity for Medications

Side effects

I returned to the United States in October of 2005. My parents were as relieved as I was when I returned from Australia. I visited my psychiatrist soon after my return. He continued to prescribe the same medications I had been taking prior to my initial trip to Australia. My psychiatrist also prescribed an anti-psychotic, because of my suicidal ideations. He reinforced my desire to become mentally stable by explaining to me, once again, my bipolar disorder required medications. I understood this fact and with new determination took my medications as prescribed.

Christmas was without incident that year, due to my commitment to regain mental health. My parents and I flew to see Brad in Tampa. We all went to Busch Gardens and road the roller coasters. My parents paid the bill for dinner on Christmas Eve, and returned to their hotel room. Brad and I did not stop at a liquor store on the way to his home. I refrained from getting drunk and was pleased with the result. Midnight Mass was a pleasant affair.

I was feeling much more myself when New Year's Day of 2006 arrived. My psychiatrist suggested I start seeing a therapist during my next visit. I took his recommendation and reference. The therapist was helpful. We talked about my past and he gave me suggestions on how to deal with my drastic mood changes.

He also recommended I apply for disability with the Social Security Administration.

The therapist told me Social Security disability benefits would help with my lack of financial security and health insurance, since I was having difficulties remaining employed. My parents were paying for every visit to my therapist, psychiatrist, and for medications. My burden, as I felt it was, cost my mother and father two-thousand dollars a month. My mind was overwhelmed with guilt and I often told my parents I would stop my medications in order to save them money. I grew to realize that was not an option, so I applied for Social Security disability benefits. I believed my family would no longer be burdened with the cost of my illness.

I was told a letter from a psychiatrist, which explained my mental illness, was required for consideration when I applied for disability benefits. My psychiatrist was accommodating and sent a detailed letter of my bipolar disorder and self-mutilation to the Social Security Administration. It did not take long for the Social Security Administration to grant me disability for mental illness. I went to the Social Security Administration offices to sign the finishing paperwork and met with the woman who was familiar with my case file. I was more than embarrassed, due to her awareness of my self-destructive behaviors. I reflected to myself, while sitting across from her, "she must think I'm a monster!" It was a truly humiliating experience.

I was able to work part-time and receive Medicaid from the Social Security Administration. My only concern was to save my parents money. My father was retired from the Air Force and the surgery of my severed hand cost my parents $150,000. I often thought upon the life my parents could have been living if it were not for my self-mutilation. This rumination always caused me further depression. I insisted on paying for the twenty thousand dollars I spent in Australia. My parents had already come to the same conclusion.

I looked for part-time employment after receiving disability. I acquired a job working in the materials department of a home-building supply business. I lifted eighty-pound bags of concrete all day. I did not wear my prosthetic on the job, since it required a great deal of heavy lifting. I had to wrap my stump and left hand under each bag, in order to lift the eighty pounds of dead weight. The concrete always slipped within my grasp while handling the heavy bags. Further, my stump developed a terrible rash from the concrete. I told my manager I had to quit the job after only a week.

I met a woman who was buying materials during my last day on the job. She was beautiful, with a funky quality. I professed that I was really a singer at heart while helping the woman with her purchases. She replied she sang as well. The woman told me her name was Jill and invited me to one of her shows. Jill said she would be singing at a hotel later that evening. I told her I would be there.

I was very impressed with Jill's performance that night. She sang songs in a 'Karaoke' style setting and her voice was amazing. Jill excelled at her craft. She had polished her act and entertained the patrons in the hotel bar very well. The crowd was small, but Jill performed as if there were five-hundred people present. I decided to ask Jill if the guests were allowed to sing and she kindly invited me to perform for the patrons.

I proceeded to sing one of my Broadway show tunes, accompanied by a compact disk that a piano player had recorded for me. It was the first time I attempted to sing in front of an audience since the loss of my right hand. Performing again caused me to become hypomanic, as it had during my career as a singer. My hypomania always attracted people to me. Jill was no different.

I experienced a period of rapid cycling, even though I was taking my medications as prescribed. Jill was pleased by my plethora of energy until my mania state of mind ceased to exist. The antidepressants were not assisting with my depression. The side effects of my medications caused me to become impotent as well. I was rarely able to perform sexually while with Jill. This fact frustrated me and caused Jill to think I did not find her attractive. Further, my intolerable mood swings ended our relationship after only two months. I began to truly believe a normal life was to be unattainable, due to my inability to maintain employment or personal relationships.

My psychiatrist and I never discontinued in our search to discover the most effective combination of medications, however. He continued to prescribe three of my mood stabilizers and we tried many new antidepressants. However, none of the antidepressants helped with my depression and the side effects were difficult to tolerate. Some of the medications caused me to gain a great deal of weight and I started to lose my hair.

I could not control my mood-swings, or suicidal ideations without medications, so I tolerated the side effects. I shaved my head every few days, which solved part of the problem. I slept most of the day and rarely ate. My depression only increased when I lacked the desire and energy to exercise. I decided to search for employment after five months of stagnation. I looked for a job, which might get me out of the house and create a schedule for my dreary life.

I was employed at a health club in Santa Fe in August of 2006. The pool I had worked at when in college hired me as their lifeguard manager. I worked part-time and did well in the job. The health club proved to be conducive to my mental health. The atmosphere was usually stress-free. I did not wear my prosthetic while working and the adult patrons rarely inquired as to how I lost my right hand. The curiosity of the children was expected and it did not affect me too greatly when they asked questions about my missing hand.

The indoor pool was quiet in the winter. I was the only lifeguard while on duty. I was thirty-six and took my job seriously, making three rescues during my employment at the pool from 2006-2007. I did not experience any severe depression, due to my prescribed medications and the calm surroundings of the job. The club patrons respected my privacy and this helped my state of mind tremendously.

Suicide as an Alternative

My mother and I often talked together about my periods of heavy alcohol consumption. She and I agreed Alcoholics Anonymous might be a place to make new friends who did not drink and possibly keep me from the destructive habit. I went to daily meetings, even though I did not believe myself to be an alcoholic (my inability to control my need for alcohol most frequently occurred while I was un-medicated and depressed). I respected the honesty the other people divulged and it seemed to me the alcoholic mind was similar to that of the bipolar mind...both were prone to self-destructive behaviors.

I celebrated my sixth month of sobriety in December of 2007 and eventually gained the courage to speak with a woman whom I had seen throughout my many Alcoholics Anonymous meetings. Initially, Diane and I were just friends, but soon started to date. Sex became a problem, as we grew closer. My antidepressant had sexual side effects once again. I desired to please Diane, sexually, so I discontinued my antidepressant. I became deeply depressed within two weeks. Diane and I continued to see each other, but the relationship became strained. My extreme moods affected my parents as well.

My parents were constantly worried for my safety. They did everything possible to keep me alive. However, my mother and father were exhausted by my many years of self-destructive behaviors. My parents were growing unable to disguise or hide their emotions. They both became weary and frustrated with my inability to remain medicated, to control my debilitating mood swings.

My father experienced stress driven mood swings during his career in the United States Air Force, but none too extreme considering his employment's expectations (his mother however was bipolar, Type II). My father sometimes became verbally inappropriate toward my mother without recognizing he was truly angry with me. I shouted at him with hostility on every occasion he yelled at her. I wanted to protect my mother from my father's anger, but only caused intolerable battles between the two of us. My mental health was greatly affected by our moments of hostility toward each other.

My father and I had a particularly heated discussion on January 12th of 2008. My father shouted, "You belong in a mental institution" during the argument. I lost all hope for a bright future with his angry and hurtful statement. My father's words caused me to feel useless to the world in which I was attempting to build a normal life. I was unable to quell my hate for his sentiment and raged at my father. I hit him in the head forcefully with my left fist. I was devastated by his comment and wanted him to feel pain as well.

My father and I reconciled the next day, after realizing the destruction we had caused to one another. I asked for his forgiveness and my father apologized to me for his hurtful statement. His sincerity did not help my depression however. His comment affected me deeply. I started to question myself, thinking, "Do I belong in a mental institution?" The depression I had fought so hard to combat was again overwhelming my mental health. I called my psychiatrist and visited him the next day.

My psychiatrist prescribed the same medications, but increased the dosage of my antidepressant. I had not told him I stopped my antidepressant two weeks earlier. I was determined to take my medications as prescribed while driving to the pharmacy, where upon I handed the clerk my prescriptions. I arrived to receive my medications an hour later. I told the clerk my last name and requested my prescriptions. The clerk researched my name and handed me the many white paper bags containing my medications.

There were five separate prescriptions awaiting me. She exclaimed "God, that's a lot!" My heart sank. I felt she was judging me, since I needed five prescriptions for my mental illness. I felt my bipolar disorder accelerate then decelerate within my mind. My brain was chemically imbalanced and I required a great amount of assistance for improving its abnormal function.

In that moment, standing at the pharmacy counter, I did not desire to need help ever again.

I had dinner with Diane at a local restaurant later that evening. We returned to her home and I started a fire in her fireplace. It was not my parent's house, or the fateful fireplace, but it reminded me of the night I severed my hand nonetheless. The sensation of the circular saw tearing through my flesh immediately and unrelentingly entered my body. The heat of the hot coals on the end of my right arm burned and coursed within my veins. I looked down at my stump and absorbed its hideousness once again. Anguish consumed my body, heart, and mind.

I sat next to Diane while staring deeply into the wildly vibrant red and yellow flames of the fire. Diane and I did not talk as the flames played back and forth with one another. My thoughts became overwhelmingly confined by a wanted nous end and final self-destructive act. I said "good-bye" to Diane after an hour and exited her home. I immediately drove to my parent's house, entered, and said "good-night" to my mother and father. I did not wait for my parents to fall asleep.

I proceeded to my bathroom with the medications I had acquired earlier that morning and filled a tall glass of water. I started to swallow all of my prescriptions ravenously. I took the antidepressants first, followed by the four bottles of my mood-stabilizers. I drank over six large glasses of water, in order to swallow all of my medications. I exited the bathroom and entered my bedroom with a desire for my final transition and an end to life's unbearable pain. I disrobed and lay quietly in my bed... simply waiting. I was hopeful of a beautiful relief from the endless trials and my own personal struggle with insanity.

I began to projectile vomit within an hour. My mother heard my vomiting, and my parents then entered my room. She was not aware of what was occurring within me until my father noticed my empty medication bottles. My parents tried to dress me once my vomiting ceased. I was immovable however, so they called an ambulance. My mother started to rub ice over my face and body. I realized how much my mother loved me as she did so. I was in a haze of imminent unconsciousness, and immediately felt remorse for my actions, but could not speak in order to apologize.

I entered, and then exited consciousness for two days until I finally awoke to find my parents at the side of my hospital bed. I was in a state of confusion. My throat was extremely sore and I could not speak. I quickly realized there was a breathing tube inserted into my throat. I tried to pull the tube from my mouth, but a nurse was nearby to stop me.

All attempts to speak with the nurse and my parents were impossible. I was still confused, entering, and then exiting consciousness, as I lay for another day with the breathing tube in my throat. The doctor approved the removal of my life support after I regained consciousness and the ability to breathe on my own. My throat was raw. I lay in my hospital bed for another two days.

My parents comforted and supported me while I was in the hospital. My mother was distant, however. My father was concerned about the possible damage I may have caused to my brain and vital organs, due to the overdose. I was simply confused. A week passed when the doctor told me I was going to be taken to a psychiatric hospital after my discharge from the hospital. I did not want to go to a psychiatric institution, but had no choice. Two emergency medical technicians drove me to the psychiatric hospital in Las Cruces, New Mexico later that evening.

The ambulance transport to Las Cruces was a five-hour commute. I was strapped to a gurney as I sat and stared into the glowing headlights, streaming through the rear window of the ambulance. We stopped for fuel and I purchased a ham sandwich from a deli. I attempted to speak with the driver while painfully eating my sandwich, but my throat was still very irritated. He was a nice man. The emergency medical technician asked me why I was going to a psychiatric unit. I briefly told him about my past and he was apologetic, regarding the difficult journey that lay ahead of me. We arrived in Las Cruces late into the evening, where upon I was transferred into the custody of the psychiatric hospital.

Being the new person on the block was always difficult, but especially so in a psychiatric institution. The other patients stared at me with bewilderment as I entered the facility. I was processed into the hospital for an hour and then shown to my room. It was ten p.m., but I could not sleep. My roommate snored loudly as I lay in bed staring at the ceiling. I wondered to myself "is this what my life has become?" I knew my own actions had caused me to be in such a place, but the reality of my self-destruction was present while staring into the oblivion of the textured, white ceiling tiles of my psychiatric hospital room.

XVII. Learning How to Live

Institutionalized

The psychiatric hospital was well staffed. I interacted with the hospital personnel only during my confinement. The other patients in the hospital had a similar diagnosis as mine, but I felt I did not have anything in common with them. In addition, they were highly medicated. They roamed the halls of the hospital without purpose. I declined the heavy sedatives the staff desired for me to take, in order to remain lucid. The ability to learn about my illness was given to me, and I made good use of my time.

The hospital psychiatrist met with me during my second day. We talked about my past for an hour and, upon leaving her office, she handed me some reading material. I met with a therapist later that day. She gave me more literature about my illness while I was in her office. The therapist was a very intelligent and an attractive woman with a beautiful smile. I was embarrassed she was aware of my self-mutilation and self-destructive inclinations. The therapist and I met three days later and I acquired more literature about my bipolar disorder.

I spent two weeks reading literature in the psychiatric hospital. I studied all of the material I had been given, concerning bipolar disorder, from nine a.m. until nine p.m. My psychiatrist in Santa Fe had given me much information about my illness, but my mind was unable to focus on his sound advice. I had nothing but time to read and learn while in the psychiatric hospital. I absorbed the reading material as if my very life depended upon it.

The literature on cognitive behavioral therapy gave me many tools to change my thoughts before acting on a life-threatening decision. I learned the behavior of suicide could be changed with a different thought process than I possessed. I began to understand the goal of cognitive behavioral therapy. I discovered I had the power to interrupt an unhealthy thought by making a conscious choice to replace it with a healthy one. Ruminations about severing my own hand did not have to result in suicide. The thought I could learn from the events of Christmas Eve of 2001 and live a long productive life was truly liberating.

Motherly Advice

I had a chance to speak with my parents on the telephone during the evening hours while in the psychiatric hospital. My father talked with me at length as I told him about my progress. My mother spoke to me for a short amount of time and proclaimed she was angry at my suicide attempt. I told her about my readings and explained I was learning a great deal. My mother bluntly stated she wanted something within me to change. She further explained she and my father loved and supported me for years, but I still chose to attempt suicide. Finally, she asked me to stay at the psychiatric hospital for as long as I was able to.

My mother explained her anger with me during another phone call later that week. She said neither her or my father could understand why I had not asked for help when feeling suicidal.

My mother told me I had a loving family to talk with, but chose to say "good night" and over-dose on medications.

My mother told me she was exhausted and could not make me want to live. She wanted me to learn the tools on how to survive my life while in the hospital. I replied I was trying to do so and would continue to read about my mental illness upon my release from the psychiatric hospital. This comment did not ease my mother's mind however. She kept saying, "What is different now than after your first suicide attempt?" I spent the remainder of my institutionalized days pondering a possible answer to my mother's question.

I did not want to hear or internally digest my mother's anger with me, but needed to. I attempted to learn all I could by reading every day, to never return to another psychiatric hospital. I read every piece of literature the staff recommended for me while in the facility. I worked very hard to gain the necessary knowledge about my bipolar disorder. The facility discharged me after ten days. My parents drove from Santa Fe to the psychiatric hospital in order to drive me home.

We left the psychiatric hospital and travelled the five hours back to Santa Fe. My parents and I talked about the necessity for a change in my behaviors during the drive. My mother was supportive, but still angry about my suicide attempt. She told me I needed to find a reason to live. I explained to my parents about the knowledge I had gained from my readings in the hospital and told them what the literature meant to me. I asked my mother for a "clean-slate." She was quiet most of the drive, but agreed to allow me the opportunity to practice what I had learned.

I made an appointment to visit my psychiatrist the day after my release. He was very concerned about my mental health. It was difficult to tell my psychiatrist I had ceased taking my medications prior to my suicide attempt. I explained to him the new knowledge I had gained of my bipolar disorder and cognitive behavioral therapy. My psychiatrist was pleased I had learned about my bipolar disorder, but emphasized my need for medications. He continued to prescribe the same antidepressants, mood-stabilizers, and anti-psychotics. My psychiatrist recommended I visit a psychotherapist as well.

Making sincere changes to my thought process and resulting behaviors was challenging. My relationship with my mother was strained. She requested I talk through my negative thoughts with the psychotherapist. My mother asked me to speak only about the positive aspects of my life with her. My father understood my need to talk through the painful memories of my past. He listened intently as I talked about my severed hand and suicide attempts. My father and I grew close after my discharge from the psychiatric hospital. However, I understood my need for professional assistance.

I talked with my psychotherapist about my self-mutilation in February. Cindy listened intently as I told her, in detail, the story about severing my own right hand. I needed to release the emotions of my self-mutilation, so I talked about the circular saw on every occasion I was in Cindy's office. I talked through the intense pain it caused me, both mentally and physically. Cindy was a Somatic psychotherapist. She explained I was suffering from trauma, due to the manner in which I had severed my hand.

I told her about my phantom pains, so Cindy started to work through those sensations with me. She taught me ways to release the physical pain. I was amazed with the results we achieved. Cindy told me to practice the exercises when alone, or even in a crowded room. My phantom pains decreased after only a few sessions with her.

XVIII. Acting

Budding Film Actor

I received a call from my talent agent the month after my hospitalization. I had already gained a small amount of success with film acting prior to 2008. I was cast in my first speaking role in 1997. The film was called *The Tao of Steve*, which became a popular video rental. My scene was cut from the movie, but the director assured me it was not due to my acting. She sent me the reel of my scene and I watched it several times, simply to make certain I was not an awful actor. I believed my performance to be adequate, so I joined the Screen Actors Guild in 1999.

I was cast in two films during 1999. The first was a low-budget film called *Unspeakable* with Dennis Hopper. I played a prison guard and shot two scenes in two days. One of my scenes was filmed with Mr. Hopper. He was a true man and gracious toward me. It was a pleasure to work with him, even though I had no lines in the scene.

I was scripted two speaking lines in my second scene. I performed well enough and my part remained in the final cut of the film. I watched the movie a year later and was pleased with my acting in the small part, especially my stunt work. The stunt coordinator told me to raise my hands, in order for them to take the blow of being thrown into the metal bars of a prison cell. I smashed my chest and face into the iron cage instead while filming the scene repeatedly. I suffered a few bruises, but knew no sound effects would be necessary in post-production.

My second film in 1999 was *Maniacs*. I was cast as a serial murderer. The director had the make-up artist paint a black widow tattoo on my baldhead. I looked wicked after she finished my make-up. I filmed late into the night with Jeff Fahey. Mr. Fahey killed me with a large knife before I was able to murder a young prostitute. The scene was extremely bloody and a great amount of fun to film. I looked forward to seeing myself being murdered on screen, but the editor cut my part due to the length of the film.

My first talent agent in Albuquerque did not call me again after the loss of my right hand. I was not in a very positive mental state, so this fact did not concern me a great deal. However, I changed agents in 2004 with the desire to secure work as an actor with a physical disability. My new agent called me regularly and I auditioned with or without my prosthetic. Acting was different without my right hand. I became more humble, because of my missing appendage and I attempted to project a more professional attitude than during my stage career.

I auditioned for a Screen Actors Guild short film in 2006. My agent sent me the lines (aka, sides) for a gay florist. I did not know how a florist, who is gay, should act or sound, but auditioned nonetheless. I was cast and thoroughly enjoyed filming my part in *New Beginnings*. I was given a chance to really act, with three scenes and many lines. The director thought I was funny. She had me wear my prosthetic in two scenes and one without. The beautiful prosthetic and tattoo on my right arm were effective in the film. I was pleased with the result when I viewed the short film at the Santa Fe Film Festival.

My career as a film actor began to gain momentum in February of 2008. My agent called and sent me the sides for an audition in Santa Fe, a month after regaining my mental health. I auditioned well and was granted a callback. The director of the film met with me for my callback. He liked my voice and black prosthetic, so the director cast me as a Robber in the film *Beer for My Horses*. My part had only six lines. I was just a day-player, but needed the boost in confidence that the role gave me. I spent days learning various depths to the character. I shaved my face and head on the day of the shoot and was ready for my close-up.

I shot my scene with Toby Keith and Ted Nugent. They were both very professional and quite comedic. The props supervisor gave me a white mask to wear before filming. The mask had a black hood attached to it. I placed the mask on my face and threw the hood over my head. I thought to myself "good thing I shaved."

We shot the scene seven times, during which my face was completely covered. This fact did not hinder my enthusiasm, however and I was grateful for the work. *Beer for My Horses* was shown in Santa Fe five months later. I viewed the film and was pleased with my strong voice during the scene. My portrayal of a convenience store robber was convincing. I enjoyed the film, but believed a major motion picture was the next step and natural evolution for my career.

I read all the books I could acquire on the subject of bipolar disorder after filming my scene in *Beer for My Horses*. I was actively searching for employment, but became obsessed with my bipolar disorder and wanted answers in order to gain a solution to my past destructive tendencies. The knowledge I gained began to equip me with new tools for battling my thoughts and behaviors.

The importance of medications was covered extensively in the literature I read as well.

My psychiatrist and I continued in our journey to discover a combination of medications, which would relieve my mind and resolve my self-destructive pattern. I secured a sales associate position with a home ware retailer in May of 2008. Sales had always been part of my life as an actor. My skills as a performer proved to serve me well throughout my employment as a sales associate.

The customers responded to my professional attitude and energy. My sales goals were always met and I liked my immediate supervisor. I worked part-time and my mental health was improving, due to the decreased amount of pressure of a forty-hour workweek. My shifts were five hours in length, so the phantom pains I experienced in the past did not greatly affect my physical health.

My attitude toward the inquiry of curious people changed as well. My support system (medications, psychiatrist, psychotherapist, and family) played a large role in my ability to react more positively when asked the question "what happened to your hand?" I always told them the carpentry story when customers asked about my missing appendage.

I was getting quite use to telling the false tale and simply went on with my day as they purchased their products and departed the store. The shelf life for my immediate depression upon hearing the inevitable question had decreased slightly in 2008. However, I experienced deep depression within my personal life. I had no passion for making new friends. I rarely ventured from my parent's home and therefore became very lonely.

My home ware supervisor was transferred to a different department in September of that year. My new supervisor was very difficult to tolerate and made my enjoyment of the job impossible. I quit after a month when more fruitful avenues of self-preservation revealed themselves. My film career began to thrive once again in October of 2008. My talent agent called with a promising audition. She was not able to e-mail me the sides since my role had no speaking lines. She further explained "Dave" would be the part I was auditioning for. My agent said the casting director wanted to simply meet and talk with me. I had little hope for the role as I drove to Albuquerque for my scheduled audition.

I entered the casting agent's waiting room and was greeted warmly by her. I was then called into a small white room in order to audition. She had me sit on a chair and simply talked with me about the film. We talked about my prosthetic as well. I revealed my beautiful black and silver arm from under the long sleeve shirt I was wearing. The casting director was filming our conversation. The interview was ending when she stated, "if cast, your scenes will be filmed with Mr. McGregor." My level of interest for the part and film increased.

My agent called a week later and told me I had been cast as Dave in *The Men Who Stare at Goats*. She told me George Clooney was acting in the film, as well as Ewan McGregor. Further, my agent said the role of Dave was important to the storyline of the movie. I was very excited to have achieved my goal of being cast in a major motion picture. I had no lines to learn, but anticipated the fortunate opportunity to act in a film with Ewan McGregor. I drove to Albuquerque and arrived at the crew parking lot early in the morning of December 4, 2008.

I was escorted to my trailer upon my arrival. I walked toward the large trailer and smiled while reading my character's name on the door. I walked to the hair and make-up trailer after dressing into my wardrobe. I had been shaving my head for the past eight years, but grew what little hair I could for the role of Dave. The make-up artist said my hair was fine and added a bit of make-up to my face. I was then escorted to the set. Ewan McGregor was already there. We were introduced and I was proud to be shaking his hand. I always respected his work and told him so.

My four scenes were also shot with an actor portraying the wife of Bob (Ewan McGregor). Bob was a writer and I was portraying his editor. Bob's wife leaves him for Dave (me) during the film. My scenes were mostly improvisational. I spent hours flirting with the actor on set to make it seem she was enamored by me on screen. I tried to think of funny stories, in order to entertain her, so she would react in a loving manner. The director seemed to be pleased with our film relationship. It was exhausting, but an excellent exercise for me as an actor.

I was directed to place Bob in a chokehold during our scene on my second day of filming. I certainly did not want to hurt him, but Mr. McGregor told me to "go for broke." The director yelled "action" and I pretended to choke Ewan McGregor. I locked my left hand around my prosthetic and allowed Mr. McGregor to do all the work. He threw himself all over the floor, struggling. Mr. McGregor made our scene look very convincing. The director said, "Cut" and I released Bob. Ewan McGregor lifted himself from the floor and immediately started to rub his throat. I was worried he was injured.

I apologized for any pain I may have caused and Mr. McGregor made light of the situation. I was concerned for my career. Ewan McGregor approached me a few minutes later and congratulated me on my acting. I was relieved and took the opportunity to become friendlier with him. The cast sat on set and joked about life later that evening. I was elated with the experience and Ewan McGregor's acting motivated me to continue working on my craft. The experience taught me a great deal about film and life. I learned it was not the size of the role I was portraying, but the quality of my work.

I was determined to secure more acting roles after completing my role in *The Men Who Stare at Goats*. My agent phoned and sent me the sides for another audition not long after finishing my part as Dave. My skills during film auditions were improving. I learnt film acting to be more subtle than when on stage. I was larger than life in musicals. I had to internalize the character much more when auditioning and acting in films.

My audition for *The Book of Eli* was decent enough to earn me the role of Tradesman. I took a beat between lines during the audition to slowly remove and then re-attach my prosthetic. The process made a beautifully subtle clicking sound. The director later told me I had been cast due to that moment during my audition. My scenes were filmed in March of 2009 on the set in Carrizozo, New Mexico. The experience was incredible and I was truly grateful to the Hughes Brothers for casting me. Unfortunately, my part was edited from the final cut of the film.

I could not see the Forest through the trees

I decided to search for other employment after my work was completed with *The Men Who Stare at Goats* and *The Book of Eli*. I secured a job with a luggage company in Santa Fe in April, 2009. The atmosphere was perfect for my state of mind. I worked alone during my shifts, so there was a lack of opportunity for personality conflicts with colleagues during my employment. The customers were curious about my missing hand, but I rarely showed my mental discomfort when a client would ask, "what happened to your hand?" I asked the patrons questions about themselves instead; in an attempt to relieve myself of the acknowledgement, I was physically disabled. My self-hatred usually occurred when the customer left the store, or after I returned home from work.

I continued in my relentless search for mental stability by visiting both my psychiatrist and psychotherapist every two weeks. My psychiatrist narrowed our search for effective medications to an antidepressant, two mood-stabilizers, and a thyroid medication. The combination was not as successful as I had hoped for. I continued to experience periods of great depression. I believed my uncontrollable and unpredictable mood changes would forever keep me from discovering a normal life and any possible contentment within myself.

The side effects of my antidepressant were difficult to tolerate and I became absolutely exhausted by the process of elimination. I grew reluctant to take my prescribed medications.

I once again discontinued all of my medications after more than ten years of experimentation, side effects, and sporadic relief from mental upheaval. I became deeply depressed within a week. Two months later, I was in the emergency room, due to another over-dose.

I consumed all of my remaining prescriptions on September 11, 2009. My father protected my medications in a locked box, but I told him I needed to refill my weekly pill containers. He gave me the bag of medications and I swallowed the colorful pills by the handful. I left a few tablets in each bottle so my father would not become suspicious. I walked from my bathroom to my parent's second story bedroom within a few minutes of doing so, and handed the bag of pill bottles to my father. I proceeded to the back yard patio and sat in the iron rocking chair... simply waiting for the medications to take my life.

I did not sit there for long. I lifted myself from the comfort of the chair instead, after discovering the desire to live from the recess of my deluded mind. I placed one foot in front of the other and walked the flight of stairs to my parent's bedroom. I told my mother what I had done. She calmly asked me to join her in their car. We drove to the hospital in Santa Fe and I walked into the emergency room entrance. I explained to the receptionist my abnormal actions and she escorted me to a hospital bed.

A nurse had me lay on the bed, which was surrounded by ten other beds. I became aware I was not the only patient in need of assistance at that moment. I understood my state of mind and body was not as urgent as those around me were, so I calmly waited for a doctor. My heart was racing because of the medications, but I remained lucid. My father arrived at the hospital, and was by my side when a doctor entered.

The doctor was present when I started to projectile vomit. My body was out of control as I continued to vomit for hours. A nurse asked me to drink a can of thick, black charcoal liquid in between vomitus episodes. My mother stood next to my bedside and encouraged me to drink the sludge. It tasted awful and soon after drinking a can of it, I would vomit. Nonetheless, I drank each can the nurse requested of me. The doctor assured my parents I had most likely purged my body of the medication's toxicity throughout the process of vomiting and intake of charcoal. I was taken to a different room that afternoon and remained there for two days.

The overdose on this particular occasion was much more traumatic for me than my prior suicide attempts, since I was awake during the entire ordeal. The incessant vomiting was exhausting, both mentally and physically. Further, I became more aware of the pain I had been causing my parents with my self-destructive behaviors during the insane process. I immediately became consumed with a desire to live for the first time.

I was discharged from the hospital after two days and taken to the psychiatric facility in Las Cruces, New Mexico. I pleaded with my mother for her compassion. My mother told me she was not angry with me. She was thankful I had come to her for assistance. Her words eased my conflicted state of mind. I willingly went to serve my much needed and deserved incarceration at the psychiatric hospital. It was a good place for me to build upon my determination to live. I once again gained as much knowledge about my mental illness as I could.

I called my parents two days before being discharged in late September. My father told me my talent agent had called with two auditions. I became resolute in my desire to discontinue my self-destructive behaviors. My parents arrived upon my release and we drove back to Santa Fe. I studied my lines for the auditions during the drive. The casting agent for one of the films needed an actor with a disability and I planned to show the director my pure talent, while embracing my physical disability and not my mental liability.

XIX. Mental Stability

A New Desire to Medicate

I scheduled an appointment with my psychiatrist once I had returned to Santa Fe. He explained the gravity of my bipolar disorder yet again during my session. My psychiatrist also said he understood my depressive moods. I told him my desire for a more effective antidepressant. I wanted to experience absolutely no depression. My psychiatrist gave me a prescription for another antidepressant and told me about the side effects. I needed some peace of mind and commented I was not concerned with the side effects.

I asked if there was a mood-stabilizer, which did not cause weight gain before leaving his office. I weighed 240 pounds at the time and was very uncomfortable with my body. He handed me a prescription for 10mg of Abilify. My psychiatrist continued to prescribe my 200mg dose of Lamictal. I decided to focus on my health, so I did not return to my luggage sales position. I became hopeful of the much-needed relief the new medication might provide. I also started to write daily. I began to create a manuscript of my life, in order to heal from my ruminations and conflicted memories.

Soon after my psychiatric appointment, I read about the possible side effects and dietary restrictions of the prescribed antidepressant. I decided to wait until my next session to take the psychiatrist's recommendation. I took my Abilify and Lamictal medications every day, however. I was not experiencing any depressive moods within a month. I felt content for the first time. I had energy, but not the extreme type I felt when manic. Further, the side effects of the two medications were tolerable. My mental health improved with every passing day.

I travelled to Albuquerque for my auditions in October. I was much healthier and felt I had performed well afterward. My agent called a week later and told me that I had been cast in one of the films. I was extremely grateful for the small part. The production was scheduled to be filmed in November of that year. The fact my career was blossoming at the same time as my mental health was not coincidental. All aspects of my life were improving as I gained knowledge and willingness to seek assistance with my bipolar disorder. I visited my psychiatrist and psychotherapist and continued to take my medications as prescribed.

I returned to see my psychiatrist a week after securing the role of Tom in *A Bird of the Air*. I explained my mental health was steadily improving and I was experiencing a respite from depression. My psychiatrist decided to discontinue our efforts in discovering an antidepressant. He explained some patients become depressed on antidepressants. My psychiatrist said it was rare, but a possibility. Further, he explained to me the mood-stabilizers I was taking were effective on depression, as well as mania.

I took my Abilify and Lamictal as prescribed and within two months was experiencing no depression or hypomania. The side effects were well controlled by my psychiatrist's keen knowledge of the two medications. I was finally becoming more stable after ten years of trying twenty-two different combinations of medications. I experienced a much-needed relief from my self-destructive and suicidal ideations.

The Men Who Stare at Goats was released in theaters in mid-November of that year. My parents and I drove to Albuquerque in order to view the film. My parents and I watched with great anticipation for my scenes. The film was hilarious and I was thrilled to see my part had made the final cut. The film was very entertaining and my scenes were palatable.

I purchased another ticket and stayed to watch the movie for a second time. I had to reconfirm my presence on film was effective. Again, the film was very entertaining. I watched my scenes and became less critical of my performance. The fact I was part of a major motion picture was truly gratifying. I was proud to be working as a professional film actor and looked forward to building upon my resume.

I was thrilled to be considered for the part in *A Bird of the Air*, even though its prerequisite was my disability. The movie was shooting in Santa Fe and in late November of 2009, my scenes as Tom were filmed. My part called for a man with a prosthetic, due to the fact Tom was an Iraq war veteran. The director was Margaret Whitton and *A Bird of the Air* was her directorial debut. Margaret was wonderful to work with and truly made the experience very enjoyable.

I had two callbacks for the Mickey Rourke film *passion play* in December. I was counting my blessings while waiting for my agent to call. I was talented enough and very fortunate for my small amount of success. My agent did not contact me for a part in *Passion Play*. I was not disappointed, however. I thought about the actor who had been cast and was pleased for him. My film career was progressing and I was much more humble in my efforts to congratulate others on their successes. "Spread the wealth" was my attitude.

Truth, yes... and Nothing but.

My mother and I occasionally talked about my past self-destructive behaviors. Her candid divulgence was extremely difficult for me process, but necessary. I was able to embrace her reflective sentiments. My mother commented she thought I would never be capable of facing the truth, regarding my past inability to cope with my mental illness.

She was truly pleased I was able to listen and positively process her need to share the inner turmoil she and my father had experienced throughout my self-destructive years. My parents always refrained from any confrontation, fearing I would become suicidal or deeply depressed. They granted me a great deal of time and understanding, concerning my bipolar disorder.

My parents witnessed my respites from depression for many years and always hoped I had turned the corner to mental health. My psychiatrist had truly attempted to translate his knowledge of my mental illness and its necessity for medications. Only I was faltering in my need to help myself. I was unable to grasp that a normal existence awaited me, if I simply digested, metaphorically and literally, my prescribed medications. Nothing within my human capacity could ever replace my right hand and I allowed this fact to consume me. However, my desire to be whole again was present. I simply was unable to understand, or clearly see a beautiful life was awaiting me.

Due to the efforts of my parents, psychiatrist, and psychotherapist, I became able to experience a true healing, regarding my bipolar disorder. Medications opened my mind to the endless love, which my family provided me and their unending support in my life. Their wisdom had always been available to me during my many years of self-destructive behaviors. I devastatingly chose to seek the alternative to life… the unquenchable and totality of nothingness.

I spent the next year writing. I kept a notepad next to my bed at night, in order to record any memories, which I felt necessary to recall and thus learn from. I typed-out all recollections of my painful past on my computer during the day. My parents were worried I would become depressed in my efforts to overcome the past, but I found the process of writing to be very healing. My physical health also improved as I gained the desire to resume exercising and implementing a better dietary strategy. I lost seventy pounds during 2010. I continued in my journey to complete, and eventually publish my autobiography as well.

A Passion for Learning

I learned, during July of 2010, the University of New Mexico hired adjunct instructors, who were professionals in the courses they desired to teach. I previously believed college level instructors needed a master's degree. I applied to University of New Mexico-Los Alamos campus in August. I submitted my professional acting resume and application for their necessity of a Theater Appreciation instructor.

Within a week, the University of New Mexico hired me. I discovered the position was reliant on student enrollment for my given course. The Dean contacted me in order to divulge my class was "not full." I replied I would teach the course for less compensation if the University of New Mexico would simply allow me the opportunity to teach the students who were registered. She agreed and my Theater Appreciation class began in late August of that year. I signed the contract and agreed upon half the amount of a full course salary.

I was extremely excited to be given the wonderful challenge of instructing college students in the craft of theater arts. I was granted the right to teach what aspects of Theater Appreciation that I deemed necessary for my students, so I decided to teach them acting.

History of the theater arts never interested me as much as the process of acting. I desired to translate my love of being on stage to my students. My syllabus was professionally composed, because of my efforts and that of the Arts Department chairperson. I arrived early and with a positive attitude when the course met for its first session.

My level of excitement grew as the students began to arrive. Eight students entered the classroom and sat before me. I began my new career with a tremendous sense of pride. I explained to the youthful students that I desired to lead them in their studies of the theater with a "hands-on" approach of appreciating the process of acting. The student's eager expressions slowly changed into expressions of disbelief upon hearing this. Undaunted and without hesitation, I continued to divulge the semester's systematic exciting journey.

I challenged my students with a simple homework assignment as our first class was nearing an end. They all acknowledged their enjoyment of watching films and television, so I asked them to discover a one to two minute monologue from their favorite movie or play. Further, I explained I would be grading them all on their efforts during the semester, and not what fellow classmates considered talent. My sentiment and professional manner of speaking eased my present student's minds.

I modeled my acting skills for the students by singing the second half of *Make Them Hear You* from *Ragtime* before they departed for the eve. My students heard me and became more interested in the course, while witnessing my true passion for performing. I was pleased by the fact only one of them dropped my Theater Appreciation course after the first class session. The seven remaining students excelled during the semester.

My impassioned instruction proved to be as effective as my stage and film presence. I was humble however, and respected my students for their dedicated efforts. In addition, I discovered that I learned a great deal of knowledge from my students during the process. I was inspired by their gracious attitude and granted each and every student exactly the grade they had all earned an A+ at the semesters end.

My career at the University of New Mexico-Los Alamos campus began with one three credit hour course. I offered three courses in the spring of 2011. Two of my three courses had enough students, so I instructed Theater Appreciation and Acting I during the spring months. The semester went well and I was gaining momentum, regarding a student base that enjoyed my classes and passionate style of teaching and learning. My

187

department chairperson and I looked toward the future and decided to add even more theater arts courses for the upcoming fall semester.

Writing my manuscript had stirred many recollections from my past. Further, I had grown weary by the intense memories of my self-destruction within the walls of my parent's home, so I moved to our cabin in the mountains that semester. I needed to live on my own and the cabin proved to cause me a great deal of stability, regarding my mental health. I looked for employment near my cabin as the summer months approached, so I could be close to my home in the serene mountains of Northern New Mexico.

Facing My Fears

I gained a part-time job at a local automotive repair establishment while living in the mountains during the summer of 2011. My duties there were very simple. I spent five hours a day mopping the greasy floors of the garage and emptying trashcans. The mindless work and mountain surroundings proved to be very therapeutic.

A customer entered the shop in early July and asked the owner if he knew of a capable carpenter. I had entertained the owner and his family at my cabin during my employment at his garage. They knew of my abilities and often commented on the beautiful work I had accomplished there. Thus, the owner recommended me upon hearing the customer's request.

The older man asked if I was able to repair the steps of his cabin's deck. I told him I would visit his mountain home later that day after completing my duties at the garage. I met with my new client at five p.m. and earned the job. I explained to him that I needed cash for materials and would begin construction the next weekend. The man agreed, gave me the amount I specified, and showed me the shed in which he kept his tools.

He did not own a circular saw, so I planned to purchase one for myself. I knew it would be very difficult for me to handle a saw again, but I became determined to reclaim my life and love for carpentry. I visited a hardware store two days later and procured my first circular saw since 200. The circular saw which I chose was much lighter than my previous worm drive saw, and possessed a built-in power brake to stop the blade from spinning rather quickly. I arrived at my client's cabin early on a cool summer morning and prepared for the task of re-building the deck's stairs.

I unpacked my tools from my vehicle and began the task I had been commissioned for. I placed my new saw on a workbench and attached its plug into the end of the long extension cord, leading to a power outlet in the garage of the home. I was determined to overcome my fears as I held the saw in my left hand and gently pulled against its trigger. The power and high-pitch roar startled me.

My pure strength of will to succeed and overcome allowed me cut across the two inch by four-inch redwood piece of pine, which rested underneath my right knee. My mind was steadfast in its resolve to conquer the task. However, this fact did not deter me from un-plugging the circular saw whenever it was not in use. Safety was my greatest concern and the successful completion of my first carpentry job since 2001 progressed beautifully. I phoned the client after finishing his stairs. The man said he would be back in the mountains later that week, in order to view my construction skills.

I went about my workweek at the auto garage when my client entered the establishment the next Wednesday afternoon. He gratefully shook my left hand. My new client proclaimed he was very pleased with my work and commissioned me to re-build his entire deck. I was filled with pride and respect for myself as I explained how I would re-construct his home's deck. The man agreed, ordered my specified materials, and had them delivered from Albuquerque that week. I spent the next two weekends truly enjoying the healing process of building at his home in the beautiful mountains of Northern New Mexico.

I returned to instruct at Los Alamos in late August. I began teaching three of the five courses I was offering while still residing at my family's cabin. I continued to embrace Theater Appreciation, and Acting I. My newfound passion for assisting students in gaining their own vocal abilities propelled my aspiration to also instruct Singing for Actors. I was creating the syllabus for my new course when I became aware I should create a syllabus for myself, in order to excel as an instructor. Thus, I wrote "Professor 101 Syllabus" which I gave to every new student. I explained if my students were expected to a maintain responsibility for their outlined course work, then I expected myself to fulfill a "contract" with every one of them. I gained a great deal of commitment and respect as the students read my contract.

Professor 101 Syllabus

By *Todd Lawson La Tourrette for* Todd Lawson La Tourrette
Course Objectives:

1. *I will instruct with Passion!* This concept is imperative, and can only be accomplished when I am passionate about the subject matter of the course I am teaching.

2. *My hope is to discover each student's goals & interests for the subject matter, in which they are enrolled.* I will do so by asking open-ended questions and listening intently to each student.

3. *I will Respect each student and their individual attributes.* I will assess what stage of knowledge each student is presently at, and expect only progress…not perfection.

4. *I will be vigilant in my efforts to gain further knowledge*, regarding the subject matter which I am instructing. I must continually study the material, and discover more effective ways to divulge new knowledge. Past experience has truly revealed that, as growth occurs within my students, so too have I gained knowledge and progressed myself. *It is impossible for me to teach, without simultaneously learning.*

5. *I must never ask a student to perform a task which I am not willing to perform myself.* I will lead by example, and model my own true desire to excel while learning.

6. I will attempt to verbally reward my students with every accomplishment they discover within them self. Positive reinforcement is a valuable and powerful tool. *Student(s) often respond with confidence in their own individual abilities, which leads to a passion for the subject matter being learned.*

7. *Have Fun*! Learning is a fascinating and exciting process. The pursuit of knowledge truly solidifies the concrete foundation for our future successes.

I will always strive to instruct with Joy in my heart...and a smile on my face!

XX. Overcoming vs. Chaos

Water

My grandparents built our family cabin in 1970, and its shallow well had always provided an abundance of clean, drinkable water. The nine feet deep well would not produce any water in October of 2011. I attempted to solve the problem for days, but finally discovered no water existed at the bottom of the shallow hole. I was unable to face a move back in with my parents, because of my haunted memories of their home, so I resolved to carry water from the nearby stream for my daily necessities.

I spent most of my days hauling seven-gallon containers full of the cold mountain water to the bathtub of my cabin when I was not teaching. The natural creek flowed down the mountain valley approximately one-hundred yards from its new destination. I was accustomed to fishing the chilly water during my youth, and the abundance of spring water truly became my lifeline for survival as a mountain man. I filled my tub every day, in order to flush the toilet and take an invigorating bath. I often thanked my late grandparents for the bathroom heater they had installed.

My toilet failed to flush in November of that year. I worked for an hour to clear the septic line with a toilet plunger. All I accomplished to do was break the seal of the toilet at its joint with the pipes leading underneath my cabin. I called a very kind plumber who cleared my more than full septic tank the next day.

I had grown accustomed to over-coming many obstacles, so I stayed at my cabin for the remainder of the week. I used the ash can, lined with a trash bag, for bathroom visits. I removed the old toilet and procured the septic pipes from below the cabin floor before departing for Santa Fe. It was a mess, but I needed the parts to purchase new pipes and their proper fittings.

I proceeded to a plumbing store, where I met my father. I told him I would install the new toilet and pipes if he would simply pay for the necessary materials. The total cost was less than three-hundred dollars. My Jeep was filled with the new toilet, pipes, and fittings as I headed back to the mountains. My father wanted to assist in any way he could, so he followed me back to our cabin.

I asked my father to relax in the cabin as I prepared to solve the problem. My task was successfully accomplished six hours later. I thought of cracking a bottle of expensive champagne over the rim as I flushed my new toilet with a gallon bucket of natural spring water. I still did not have running water, but reveled in my ability to solve the difficult toilet problem myself.

Reliving the Past

I joined my parents in Santa Fe when my brother Brad came to visit for the 2011 Christmas holidays. I had ceased my heavy consumption of beer since August of 2010 and was able to drink red wine in moderation. However, I craved a beer in the early afternoon of Christmas Eve, and immediately drove to the local liquor store to purchase a twelve pack. I consumed the dozen bottles of brew while working on my Jeep in the uncommonly warm December sunshine. I was intoxicated before the bright glow of day had departed. Subsequently, the celebration that evening was anything but joyous.

My brother Brad and I became strained with one another that evening. He questioned my inability to escape the endless ruminations, concerning the loss of my right hand. I resented his lack of support or understanding. However, we were able to act civilly towards one another during most of the afternoon. The gates of hell flew open on the night of December 24, 2011 and I gladly entered there in.

I fried two chickens for an enchilada dinner as the sun was setting over the westward Jemez Mountains. I spent two hours cooking and drinking more alcohol. I asked Brad what sized portion he would like to have after completing the dinner. He told me he did not want any of my enchilada. Further, he walked into the pantry and prepared himself a bowl of breakfast cereal. I became outraged and in my drunken state was unable to conceal my anger. What transpired next was nothing less than pure chaos.

I began shouting at my brother, who then retorted loudly "is Christmas Eve your day?" My father then yelled at Brad and me. My mind lacked all capability of reasoning with my desire to self-destruct as my family continued to argue. I walked upstairs without the ability to rationalize. I grabbed my mother's scissors and started cutting deeply into my body. Brad attempted to stop me, but was unable to. A familiar calm fell upon me as the blood began to flow over my chest. I then shattered the glass of two large paintings that my mother had created.

My mother then told me she had called the police after I returned downstairs. Total consumption entered my entire being. I knew the police would find me most guilty of any wrongdoing, and forcefully take me from my parent's home. I understood all too well the fate that awaited me at the nearby hospital. Further, I would be admitted into the same Santa Fe hospital on the exact fateful night where I had been ten years before due to the brutal severing of my own hand. I lost all control before the police arrived and threatened to kill myself with a knife, which I had grabbed from the utensil drawer.

My father entered my peripheral view a moment later and began to spray my entire face with mace. I ran from him, but he pursued and continued to cover my entire body with the burning discharge. The container was empty when I dropped to the floor and submission overcame my self-destructive spirit. The police arrived and immediately asked me to exit the premises. I requested to wash my face and body before leaving. They allowed me to and I cleansed myself. The burning sensation increased in intensity as the police escorted me from the judgmental eyes of my family.

I had hours to reflect upon the insane events of the night as I sat on my bed of the emergency room. I quietly and convincingly lied about what had occurred when the doctor entered. In addition, I told her of my true need to leave the hospital as soon as was possible.

My flesh was burning intensely, but I remained calm. She listened intently as I divulged the carpentry story and inability to be in the same hospital on the exact night of my "accident" ten years prior. Little did I know my parents had already called the hospital and talked with the physician. They had requested she admit me into their psychiatric ward.

Nonetheless, my lies were very convincing and the doctor discharged me of my own accord thirty minutes later. I booked a taxi to drive me to my parent's home. I called my father on route.

He told me I was not welcome to stay and he had already packed the Jeep for my return to the mountains that night. The cab dropped me off in front of my parent's home where my father was waiting. He handed me my keys to the auto and I departed.

I arrived to the cabin at four a.m. I laughed insanely during the drive due to my father's reaction of spraying me with mace. I displaced any judgment upon my father for his action, however. Instead, I understood that he truly loved me… as did my entire family. I knew my many years of self-destructive behaviors had exhausted their ability to be complacent. I called my father when I arrived safely at our family cabin.

I began unpacking my vehicle and found the inside temperature of my cabin to be only five degrees Fahrenheit. I promptly started a fire and ignited the wall furnace, in an attempt to warm myself. I carried thirty gallons of water from the back of my Jeep and poured them into the bathtub. I spent the early morning hours listening to music until the radiance of a new day became prevalent with the oncoming glow of sun light.

I called my father a few hours later and wished him a merry Christmas. I told my family I was all right and I loved them. We exchanged a few kind sentiments and then parted from our short conversation. I could not keep myself from listening to Brad's beautiful musical creations for many days thereafter. His music truly kept me warm and less lonely. He and I soon after reconciled, and attempted to build upon our friendship once more.

A Hand, a Hand! My Kingdom...

I threw myself back into work diligently and wrote new syllabi for the previous courses I had been instructing. I also made an appointment to visit my primary care doctor before the spring semester of 2012 began, because of an extreme pain in my left shoulder. I drove to Santa Fe after the New Year had passed and met with my doctor. I explained the severity of the pain I was experiencing in my left arm and shoulder. He handed me a prescription for an MRI.

I immediately drove to Santa Fe Imaging and scheduled an appointment. Images of my left shoulder and bicep were created the following day. My doctor called a week later and suggested I see a specialist for a second opinion. I agreed and was in the waiting room of an orthopedist surgeon within days of my doctor's suggestion.

The orthopedic surgeon reviewed the result of my MRI. He explained that I had a torn rotator cuff, and detached bicep in my left arm. He further recommended I have surgery. I asked what type of recovery was to be expected from such a surgery. The man replied I would not have the full use of my left arm for weeks, if not months. He then looked upon my missing right hand. I smiled as he and I both realized the process would be difficult. We discussed my special circumstances, but the orthopedic surgeon truly believed that surgery was the best option if I desired to regain the use of my left arm well into the future.

Only two of the five courses I was offering at the University of New Mexico-Los Alamos had enough students for the spring semester. This fact did not cause me any type of stress, however. My upcoming surgery in February was of paramount concern to me instead. I was teaching Acting Acting II and I. I called my Dean on February 1st and explained the need to cancel classes for the week after my surgery. She understood and wished me the best, regarding a speedy recovery. My parents kindly accompanied me to the Northern New Mexico Orthopedic Center in Santa Fe for my scheduled surgery on February 9, 2012. I departed many hours later with my immovable left arm in a sling.

I arrived at my parent's home and sat in the brown recliner, which my father had purchased, for my post-surgery recovery. My surgeon had previously explained recliners were best suited to sleep in after a surgery of my type. The pain in my shoulder was intense, so I asked my parents for a dose of the prescribed pain medications. I fell asleep once the pills had become fully digested. A few hours later, I awoke and requested another dose. I regulated my pain medications as prescribed, but lived hour by hour with the intolerable circumstances of my situation.

My pre-surgery mind-set was focused on accomplishing many tasks, in order to care for myself while lacking the use of hands. I created a fork and spoon attachment for my prosthetic, so I could feed myself. I designed and built two other tools that would allow me to dress myself. I even created a customized leather sling. I prepared for every possible obstacle. However, what I failed to create within my prideful mind was the desire to ask my parents for their help. Blood had pooled inside the skin around my left bicep and shoulder after only forty-eight hours of my surgery.

The surgeon prescribed another MRI after he witnessed the state of my post-surgery left arm. The resulting images required another surgery to repair the damage I had caused. My surgeon explained I had somehow torn a second rotator cuff, along with the one he had previously repaired. He went on to state I had completely pulled the screw from my humorous bone that he had firmly secured, in order to re-attach my left bicep. Finally, the man explained if I damaged this new bout of surgery, he would be unable to further repair my shoulder.

I returned to the Northern New Mexico Orthopedic Center two weeks later. A nurse mocked me a bit before my surgery. My gracious surgeon was not upset I had destroyed his work, however. He showed compassion instead, regarding my challenging and difficult process. I departed in a painful haze later that evening and headed home with my parents.

I desired a full recovery, so I decided to rely on my parents for assistance. My mother and father provided a great deal of necessary help and mental support throughout the following two months. My mother prepared my meals and assisted me while eating. My father drove me to Los Alamos for my class sessions at the University of New Mexico. My students witnessed my positive attitude as I stood before them without the use of hands. I continued to instruct with passion. I remained gainfully employed and mentally driven to survive the ordeal.

I never contemplated any type of self-destruction during my recovery. I whole-heartedly built upon my desire to live by creating a viable path to overcome any obstacle and plan to strive throughout my daily challenges. I finished the spring semester armed with my newly discovered ability to thrive in the face of adversity. This fact often revealed itself to my students and colleagues. My career as an instructor thrived, along with myself. My status as an effective teacher began to gain recognition.

However, in the light of new opportunities and a rejuvenation of mental health… I consciously crossed the boundary between self-preservation and self-destruction by discontinuing my prescribed medications once again.

XXI. New Opportunities

Old Habits

I resided with my parents while teaching the summer session in Los Alamos. The cabin still produced no water and my ability to carry heavy loads from the mountain stream was impossible. I was finally able to drive myself to the Los Alamos campus for my class sessions after three months of relying on my father. I entered the Community Education building as the semester progressed and asked if they were in need of a German instructor.

The department chairperson seemed open to my suggestion and asked me to forward an e-mail of my University of New Mexico transcripts. She also requested I create an outline for the possible course. I sent her my newly created German 101 syllabus the next day, as well as my university transcripts. The credit/no-credit course was approved and scheduled to be taught by me in the fall.

The Community Education department Chairwoman asked me to select a German textbook from which to instruct and offer to students. I researched many and chose *Neue Horizonte,* due to its English translation of "New Horizons." I truly needed such inspiration, since I had no horizons while continuing to discontinue my prescribed medications. However, I promptly phoned the publisher and requested an instructor's copy of the text. Soon after, a man from the Santa Fe Community College left a message on my cell phone. He asked me to return his call as soon as I was able.

I called the World Languages department chairperson at the Santa Fe Community College later that day. He explained the college had an urgent need for a German language instructor. The man had called the University of New Mexico the previous week and learned I was to be instructing German 101 in Los Alamos. Thus, he acquired my phone number. He then asked me to instruct the fall semester of German 111: Introductory German. I was honored to join the dedicated faculty and staff of the Santa Fe Community College a few weeks later.

The German 101 course that I was instructing at the University of New Mexico was ten weeks in length and met every Monday evening for two hours. The course at the Santa Fe Community College was seventeen weeks long and the class met for three hours per week. I had been continuing to learn German since my studies of the language during my degree. However, I knew teaching the language to twenty-three students was going to be challenging and require me to continue my studies of German with verbosity.

I decided to create PowerPoint presentations to instruct from, after looking upon the *Neue Horizonte* text. I created over 420 color presentations. I often slept only four hours per night during my employment as an adjunct German instructor. I usually woke in the early morning hours, in order to create new presentations for my eager students and my own desire to learn. I was experiencing the type of hypomania I had grown accustomed to during my past bouts with productive sleeplessness. However, I was also truly dedicated to teaching and learning.

I was instructing four courses in Los Alamos during the fall semester. I eventually moved into an apartment in Los Alamos, because of my many class sessions at the University of New Mexico and travelled to Santa Fe twice a week for the German 111 course. The department chairperson for the Communication and Journalism department contacted me halfway through the fall semester and asked if I was willing to teach a three credit hour course in German for their Los Alamos campus during the spring semester. Further, she was hoping I would instruct the Public Speaking course during the next semester as well. I was flattered and stated I would be honored.

My Santa Fe Community College German 111 students and I learned the language well by the semesters end. I told them I was attempting to offer German 112 in the spring, and we parted company after I administered their final examination in mid-December. My instruction with the University of New Mexico was also completed as the students prepared for the holidays. I had always enjoyed my month's break at Christmas during my bachelor's degree. However, as an adjunct faculty I knew my days prior to the 2013 spring semester were to be filled with preparation for the three new courses I was to be offering.

Self-love

I continued to instruct my Theater Arts courses and began teaching Public speaking while also teaching German 101 in Los Alamos for the spring semester. Enrollment in the German 112 course at the Santa Fe Community College had gained enough students from my previous German 111 class, so I continued to drive to Santa Fe twice a week. Sleep was a rare commodity for me during the spring semester. The lack of my prescribed medications did not assist with my sleep patterns, or my waning ability to rationalize clearly.

I soon became exhausted... physically, mentally, and emotionally. The fact I was earning very little capital as an adjunct faculty member was detrimental to my rational to continue teaching as well. I was compensated an average of twelve-thousand dollars per year since my instructional career began. I was dedicated, passionate, and truly honored to be teaching. However, I was growing more and more disillusioned with my financial status. Thus, I hastily decided to re-enter the acting profession on stage. I resigned from the University of New Mexico and Santa Fe Community College in May of 2013 with the desire to fulfill my own creativity in New York City once again.

I departed from the University of New Mexico after completing my instructional responsibility of University 101 in August of 2013. University 101 was another course that a colleague had requested of me to instruct. She witnessed my true passion and dedication for the Los Alamos students, and asked me to teach the summer session. I agreed, and completed my contract with the University of New Mexico by guiding its students into their own awareness of self-love and limitless abilities to survive... against all odds. They were unaware I had already departed from such inspirational concepts months prior, if not many years before hand.

XXII. Past, Present...Future

Honesty and Forgiveness

I shall divulge the remainder of my autobiography with the very same honesty that I have translated thus far. My memory of the past has been clouded by the chaos of my existence. I am unfortunately unable to recall the many beautiful moments of my life. I have truly embraced the horrors instead. I am uncertain as to whether my mind has disposed of its joy purposefully, or if I am unconsciously attempting to learn my necessary lessons as a survival instinct.

I have had, and continue to have selfless moments for those I love. My parent's home and our family cabin are a testimony to my efforts as a skilled carpenter over the past twenty years. I continue to beautify their house, even though my left shoulder and bicep have never fully healed, or become very useful to me. I use my stump to handle the heavy lifting and work (even though it has suffered the same injuries. My right bicep is detached, as well as two torn rotator cuffs). I am still able to accomplish most tasks that many people take for granted.

I often pondered throughout my four years of instructing at the University of New Mexico and the Santa Fe Community College whether I was qualified for the positions of which I held. However, I never questioned my dedicated efforts to learn and teach. I simply believe perhaps my bipolar disorder and lack of ability to properly treat my mental illness disqualified my role as an educator. My behavior in the classroom was always professional. I only failed my students when off-stage.

Romantic love has eluded me for most of my life. I have had lovers. However, none of them has ever fully displaced my memories of Laura in Las Vegas. Laura was, and continues to be my first and last true love. I know her ability to return my affection is nearly impossible. I am certain she has created what I have most often destroyed... *peace* within herself.

I possess very few friends, but my desire to assist others is unwavering. My inability to care for myself has truly been the catalyst of my own self-destructive past.

My conscious decision to discontinue my very necessary prescribed medications during my adult years has absolutely destroyed the innocence within me. My boyhood is but a distant memory. My mother often talks to me about the blissful childhood that I enjoyed. I love to listen as she reminisces upon my humor, playful smile, and purity of heart. I have no recollection of these traits within me. I continue to strive for a life in which I am not the monster whom I have come to know myself as.

I have truly exhausted my every resource while writing and surviving this manuscript. My parents were and remain to be very concerned I will self-destruct, due to my endless efforts to divulge my conflicted past. My need to heal has been first and foremost in my conflicted mind, broken body, and soul. I have accomplished my arduous task if my autobiography helps only one person to circumvent the same journey that I have chosen.

My ability for self-preservation has very often been effective in displacing the truths in my life. Today I attempt to fully grasp the fact I, Todd Lawson LaTourrette, am bipolar. I brutally severed my own right hand while experiencing a psychotic mixed episode on December 24th of 2001. My body is strewn with visible scars. My desire for the hypomania of a tattooing needle has never departed from my base needs (all of my tattoos are designed and dedicated to the love I have for my mother and father, however).

I have told many lies throughout my life, without the ability to discontinue my web of untruths to others and myself. This fact is due to my misunderstanding of how I can survive the discourse that I have created myself. I simply do not possess the skills to live a normal existence. My learning curve has been hindered by my inability to swallow the truth...metaphorically and literally.

My place of residence has changed with the ensuing mania and depression, which followed my discontinuation of medications in May of 2013. I first moved to New York City where I remained for only a month. I then moved to Las Vegas, Nevada. I lost all hope within two months of relocating there and over-dosed on the entirety of my prescriptions once again. I obviously did not succeed with my suicide attempt. All I accomplished was further mental anguish and self-abasement.

My film and television career continues to thrive somehow (Owen Lauterbach in the ABC television series *Killer Women*, Ben Fulsom in the CW's *The Messengers*, a Rockabilly bartender in A&E's *Longmire*, and a Drifter in the WGN America's *Manhattan*). However, I was primarily cast in *The Messengers* due to my finely tuned ability to tell untruths convincingly. The television show was in need of a disabled Afghanistan veteran. I regretfully told producers, directors, and casting agents I had suffered and survived a similar fate as a Private Military Contractor in the region overseas.

I did so due to my need for acceptance, employment, and financial security. I am haunted by telling this untruth, while dishonoring the many veterans whom have fought bravely for the freedoms of which I am able to comfortably live. My transgression came to fruition because of my desire to be viewed as a hero to those whom ask, "What happened to your hand?"

My cowardly lie has altered my own reality. I truly do not wish to be Todd at times. I want to have honor, dignity, and pride within myself. However, I simply do not believe I possess these beautiful attributes. I am not a veteran of foreign war who fought the Taliban forces in Afghanistan. I am at war on United States soil...with myself. The M-4 Carbine rifle is not the weapon I choose to fight my battles with. No, my weapons are a circular saw, hand-full after hand-full of psychotropic drugs, and pair of scissors or sharp knife.

I do love my endlessly supportive and caring family very much. My relationship with my brother Brad has truly blossomed. His beautiful music is extremely inspirational, and he is very generous to share such creativity with me. Brad's gracious spirit has truly translated to his children. His sons are just as beautiful as Brad and his ability to create wonderful pieces of musical artistry.

My brother Scott has embraced his wonderful family's need for stability with unending support. He is selfless in his unquestionable abilities to provide a safe and loving home. His family has sacrificed much for one another. They have overcome and endured many obstacles. Scott's children are a testimonial of their own giving qualities as well, through extremely difficult hardships and trials. They too are inspirational, regarding their abilities to survive and thrive through the face of adversity.

There truly exists no possible manner to fully translate the love I feel for my parents. Their endless support and love has been integral to my very survival. They have been through hell and back as passengers in the insane journey of my life. My mother and father have conflicted emotions, concerning my publishing of this manuscript, however. My parents feel my past may be harshly judged by the public eye. What they are unaware of is the fact I have already been harshly judged… by myself. I need closure, regarding my past. I need and desire for others to know the truth of why I have no right hand.

My family is deeply concerned for me whenever I experience a more than normal mood-swing. I am aware of their desire for my complete mental recovery. However, I truly believe this desire to be unattainable. One of my favorite books is the English dictionary. Thus, I recently looked for two definitions. The Webster's New Compact Desk Dictionary defines the term "complete" as "2. to make whole or perfect." The same dictionary defines "perfect" as "1. complete in all respects; flawless." I am finally able to realize these definitions, concerning my human mind and body, are not applicable to my conflicted mind and disabled body.

I am Todd Lawson LaTourrette. I am imperfect, incomplete and consumed by my past self-mutilation and destructive behaviors. I have been committed to taking my daily prescriptions since May of 2014. I did swallow my medications this morning, with hope in my heart for a brighter future. I truly desire to wake tomorrow morning with air in my lungs and the strength to take the colorful pills again. Inhalation to exhalation is all I have. I no longer wish to destroy myself. Instead, my mind is consoled with thoughts of a possible modicum of peace in my life.

My newly discovered desire and ability to visit my psychiatrist before self-destructing has now become the road on which I travel for my very survival. I truly desire an existence free of ruminations and self-abasement. I have become exhausted by self-hatred for my own daily reflection in the honesty of a mirror, while simply brushing my teeth or shaving my scarred face. I hope those I have hurt, lied to, or taken for granted will forgive me. I will resume my journey by attempting to forgive myself.

The beginning...